BELLY LAUGHS

BELLY LAUGHS

*the naked truth about
pregnancy and childbirth*

Jenny McCarthy

Da Capo
LIFE
LONG

A Member of the
Perseus Books Group

Designed by Jeff Williams
Set in 11-point ITC Garamond by the Perseus Books Group

Cataloging-in-Publication data for this book is available from the Library of Congress.

First Da Capo Lifelong Books edition 2004
ISBN 0-7382-0949-X

Published by Da Capo Lifelong Books
A Member of the Perseus Books Group
http://www.dacapopress.com

Da Capo Lifelong Books are available at special discounts for bulk purchases in the U.S. by corporations, institutions, and other organizations. For more information, please contact the Special Markets Department at the Perseus Books Group, 11 Cambridge Center, Cambridge, MA 02142, or call (800) 255–1514 or (617) 252–5298, or e-mail special.markets@perseusbooks.com.

1 2 3 4 5 6 7 8 9—08 07 06 05 04

To Evan —

the little man who changed Mommy's world.

Thank you for filling my soul with giggles and

allowing me to experience the kind of love

I had only read about in fairy tales.

You are my sunshine.

Contents

So You Got Knocked Up? (Getting Pregnant)   1

Honey, Your Sperm Really Do Work!
(Pregnancy Tests)   5

Barf-O-Rama (Morning Sickness)   9

Niagara in My Pants (Vaginal Discharge)   13

Psycho Chick (Hormonal Rage)   15

Holy Shit, I Think I Hard-Boiled My Baby!
(Taking Hot Baths)   19

Granny Panties (Letting Go of the G-String)   23

I Can Either Pee on You or You Can Get the Hell
Out of My Way! (Frequent Pee Breaks)   27

Passing Stonehenge (Constipation)   31

Is It a Penis or a Vagina? (Finding Out the Sex) 37

Can I Have a Mustard Sandwich with
Pickles, Anchovies, Peanut Butter, and a
Little Cottage Cheese? . . . Oh, and Throw
a Few Fish Sticks on There! (Cravings)   43

Where in the Hell Can I Find a Muumuu?
(Nothing to Wear)   47

Freddy Krueger Ain't Got
Nothing on Me! (Dreams)   53

Is That an Apple on Your Rectum,
or Are You Just Happy to See Me? (Hemorrhoids)   57

Hi, Porn Star! (Engorged Breasts)   59

Ready and Squeeze . . . Your Kegels
(An Exercise for the Vagina)   65

Well, It's Not 1972 Anymore! (Baby Boomers
Explaining How It Was in Their Day)   69

Did a Sewer Tank Explode,
or Did You Just Fart? (Gas)   73

Hands Off, Dude! (Strangers Touching Your Belly)   75

I Can't See! I'm Bleeding! I Can't Stand It!
(Weird and Painful Bits and Pieces)   77

www.ihavetostopbuyingbabyshit.com
(On-Line Baby Stores)   81

Is It Hot in Here or Is It Just Me? . . . It's Just Me
(Hot Flashes and Fainting Spells)   83

Oh, Oh, Oh, Oh, OOOOOOOOHHHHHHH! . . .
I'll Take Another One of Those, Please!
(Orgasms in Pregnancy)   87

The Crying Game (Hormonal Blues)   91

So, Anyway, Like I Was Saying . . .
Wait, What Was I Saying? (Wandering Mind)   95

Mirror, Mirror on the Wall, Who's the Prettiest
Pregnant Lady of Them All? Clearly Not You, Lady!
(Face Acne and Rashes)   97

It's a Bird! It's a Plane! . . . No, It's a
Really Swollen Pregnant Lady! (Water Retention)   101

The McRib Sandwich (Back Pain)   105

Headaches (Headaches . . . Duh)   109

That Ain't My Ass! (Cellulite Gain)   111

No, Not Yet! I'm Not Ready for This Yet!
(Premature Labor)   115

Poopin' on the Table (The Dark Side of Delivery)   119

The Blue Twinkies (Your Swollen Vagina)   123

Die, Model Bitch, Die! (Hating Skinny People)   125

OOOOH! I Think I Felt the Baby Move . . .
or Maybe It's Just Gas (Baby Kicks)   129

Organizing Freak (Your Nesting Instinct)   133

Breathing for Dummies (Lamaze)   **135**

What the Fu*k Are These? (Stretch Marks)   **139**

I Just Need to Lie Down for, Like, Five Minutes . . .
Okay, Maybe Three Months (Sleepiness)   **143**

Pig in the Pasture (Sex in the Ninth Month)   147

The Moment of Truth (Labor and Delivery)   149

Let Me Repeat (Husband No-No's)   163

So You Got Knocked Up?
(Getting Pregnant)

———————————

Though as a warning we were always told that getting pregnant was an easy thing to do, most of you know that trying to get pregnant can be a grind—not always nearly as easy as they told you back in sex ed. Still, you did the nasty and got the job done. Congratulations and welcome to the club! You're finally going to get the opportunity to fully utilize your uterus and get to know your vagina in ways that you've never imagined.

As most mothers will tell you, pregnancy is a roller-coaster ride full of laughs, cries, aches, pains, and love the likes of which you've never experienced before. But because they've either conveniently forgotten with time or they're trying to be supportive, most mothers won't tell you how hard pregnancy (and then child-birth) can be. Let me tell you, it is. It's brutal some-times! But, if I did it, ANYONE can do it. I mean, I always knew I was meant to do something really BIG in life, and now I know that this was it. Screw winning an Academy Award someday . . . I GAVE BIRTH! In my eyes, women should be adored and thanked on a daily basis for their strength, endurance, and willingness to give birth. If it were up to men to do so, Adam and Eve would have been the only humans to ever walk the face of the earth.

If you bought this book, you are already aware of my frankness when it comes to certain things—anato-my and bodily functions among them. If someone gave this book to you as a gift and you've never heard of me, apologies to you! Because pregnancy took my frankness to a whole new level. I found myself reveal-ing things about what was happening to me that most women are way too embarrassed to talk about. But what I found is what I hope you'll discover, too: It's a huge relief to know that other women are going through similar gross and smelly things. And girl, are they ever. No pregnant woman has entirely escaped the rough waters that lie ahead of you. Some got off easi-er than others, of course, but in one way or another, we've all been there. And having been there grants all of us membership in our own massive club. (Though he may be supportive and understanding, not even your male gyno can get access to our club. I mean, he's seen the process up close and really personal, but has he squeezed a watermelon through the hole in his penis to approximate the pain his patients feel? I don't think so.)

Bottom line: Brace yourself. The only silver lining to the horrific things I went through is that I can relay them here for your reading pleasure. You are going to hear me tell it like it is. Sometimes I'll make you laugh and sometimes I'll scare the shit out of you, but know this . . . I think it's in your best interest to know the full range of strange things that might happen to you. And what's more, I would do it all over again in a second, and when all's said and done, I'll bet you'll want to, too.

Honey, Your Sperm Really Do Work!

(Pregnancy Tests)

Finally, his sperm have been put to good use. His poor little fish didn't have to die in a cold rubber, drown in spermicide, or get scrubbed out of your hair. They have served their God-given purpose, and the little dipstick that can change your future has confirmed that life is indeed about to change for you. Here's how it all happened for me.

When we were "trying" to conceive, my husband and I were afraid of doing anything that seemed inappropriate during sex, like, say, uttering the slightest noise. Missionaries never had it so quiet and clean. We knew that what we were doing was creating a beautiful life, so the last thing I was going to tell my husband to do was to slap my ass and call me a naughty bitch. Our innocence seemed to have worked because weeks later I found out I was pregnant. Discovering was one of the most fun parts of the entire process.

We were traveling to New Orleans on business. Well, actually he was working. I chummed along because I hated being without him. The night we arrived we went out to eat. It was the first time I experienced a sensation that would become very familiar: that gaping hole in my stomach that was screaming for something to fill it. When we sat at the table, I asked the waiter ever so politely to bring some bread to the table immediately. There was urgency bordering on hysteria in my voice and the look on my face worried my husband. He offered me a piece of gum to hold me over and I told him to shove it up his butt. One minute passed and there was still no sign of bread. I stopped everybody who walked past our table and asked them to bring over some fucking bread. Minutes seemed like hours. But still, no bread came. My eyes filled with tears as I begged my husband to go to the kitchen and grab the bread. He knew if he didn't I was going to jump over our table to the one next to us and eat their bread. Either that or I was going to beat the shit out of our waiter.

So, off my husband went. As instructed (by him), I remained sitting at the table but by this time I was cross-eyed and becoming delirious with hunger. I stopped for a moment and thought, "Hey, maybe I have a tapeworm," but the thought didn't last long because seconds later, off on the horizon, I saw the most beautiful loaves of white bread in my husband's hands. He was my hero.

My husband got me bread! I loved him for that. Screw diamonds! I went to bed that night still worrying over tapeworm, but that was to be my last night with that particular worry. My discovery of "pregnanthood" came the next morning.

My husband left very early for work while I lay in the hotel bed complaining and whining about having cramps. Before we left for the trip my husband had bought a pregnancy test and I, ever skeptical, had bought tampons. As the morning progressed my cramps were so bad I thought for sure I was bleeding all over the place. So I grabbed a tampon and headed for the bathroom. I ripped off my underwear expecting the leftovers from the *Texas Chainsaw Massacre* only to find . . . NOTHING. I pondered for a moment as I stared at my tampon. I decided to give the tampon a second life, and I put it back in the box. I walked over and grabbed the pregnancy test my husband had been trying to get me to take. I thought, "What the hell?" As I peed on the stick I hoped I was pregnant but just "knew" that I wasn't. But as soon as I was done peeing I held up the stick and a plus sign appeared immediately. My mouth dropped to the floor and I rubbed my eyes in total disbelief. My husband's sperm totally worked and my eggs weren't rotten. Oh my God. OH. MY. GOD. I'M PREGNANT!!

I ran to the mirror just to witness the expression on my face. And you know what? I've honestly never seen myself happier. I was positively giddy! I giggled at myself in the mirror and began jumping up and down. I looked down at my belly and smiled. We had created life. I wanted to introduce myself to the embryo and tell him to enjoy the ride. And I clearly remember thinking: I'm going to be a great mom.

My husband wasn't coming back to the hotel for ten more hours and that was the longest wait in history. But the wait was worth it. I didn't want to tell him on the phone. I had to see the excitement on his face. When he walked in the door he noticed a funny look on mine. I couldn't stand it and said casually, "I'm pregnant, baby." He looked at me and his face softened. He hugged and kissed me and then he praised his sperm. He was so proud of himself. I was proud of us. We fell asleep talking about names and whose features we hoped our baby would have.

Little did my husband know what was headed his way. Not the hardships of a newborn, no. He had to get ready for the wave of craziness and sometimes hell his pregnant wife was about to experience. Follow us down that happy, hellish hole . . .

Barf-O-Rama

(Morning Sickness)

As anyone who has ever endured it knows, the term *morning sickness* is bull-shit. Morning has very little to do with it. For me, it started in the morning and went straight through the night. The label *morning* must have been thought up by a man who thought it was all in our heads and hoped that limiting the definition would make us all shut up by noon. Well, I don't think so, buddy! I say, come on over to my house around 5 p.m. so I can heave on you.

Some women I know have had this worse than others. Some have puked every fifteen minutes all day long and others just a few times a day. I consider myself to have had it even harder than the pukers. I was in a constant state of queasiness that would cause me to gag or dry-heave. You know that second before you throw up where your mouth gets really watery and you start to sweat and you do that horrible run to the bathroom hoping to just get it out so you don't have to feel that anymore? That was me . . . ALL DAY. I was stuck in that in-between state where nothing would come out. I would just stare at the toilet sweating and praying to the porcelain God not to let me dwell any longer in puke purgatory. I would have sold my soul for one of two options: Either let me puke or let me feel better.

Going to the grocery store was a freakin' nightmare. I was terrified every time I had to go. Celebrity life isn't all personal assistants and glamour, let me tell you. Oh yes, I do my own shopping. I would walk in pale and sweaty with my little list in my hand and run through the aisles. To me, the meat counter smelled like dead animals that had been left in the sun for a year. I would cringe and hold my sleeve up to my nose as I passed. Everything in that store disgusted me. Strangers gawked at me as they saw me gagging in Aisle 3 holding up some cheese. It's hard having these symptoms in public when you don't look pregnant. If I were nine months along they would look at me like "oh look, poor little pregnant lady doesn't feel so good." Instead they looked at me as if to say, "Don't bulimics puke *after* they eat?"

Television food commercials killed me. I loved them for cravings later on, but during this early stage I turned green when I saw someone eat a greasy cheese-burger or some Hamburger Helper. Speaking of green, if any type of vegetable or salad was in my vicinity (or even talked about in passing conversation), I would feel the need to eliminate the healthy little bastard. Everyone always talks about eating healthy for the baby, but the only healthy thing I ever got down in nine months was an apple. I was worried my kid was going to come out looking like a chocolate chip cook-ie. Health food DISGUSTED me.

You'd think with all this aversion to food that I would lose weight during this period . . . nope. Instead, I gained a lot. Probably because the only thing that I could get down was an entire loaf of white bread every day. As I would later find out from asking around, the people who do lose weight during "morning sickness" eventually catch up to us fat pregnant women later. Fair's fair.

So if you succumb to becoming best friends with your toilet, don't fret. Just remember you're not alone. All women are right there with ya holding your hair up, cheering you on. For most of us, it all passes in a few long months. The max is nine months, I promise.

Niagara in My Pants

(Vaginal Discharge)

Okay, like there isn't enough shit going on down there, we have to go through this, too. Ever since the day I got my period I thought, "God, I can't wait 'til I'm pregnant. I'll go through nine months of no period. Yeah!" Bullshit. Vaginal discharge—as the doctor calls it—was just as bad if not worse because it didn't come for a week and then disappear like dear old Aunt Flow. Instead, it just flowed. And flowed and flowed. At least it did for me. I called it the "snail trail" because it's gooey and slippery and nasty. And it made me feel like I had wet my pants all the time. You could be reading this right now saying, "Damn, Jenny had a real problem in this department." Good for you if you didn't discharge all day and night but, well, I did. And I'm sharing.

It drove me crazy. I went through a few pairs of underwear a day until one of my friends said, "Why don't you wear a little panty liner?" God, sometimes I am a true blond! It didn't take the annoyance away, though. I swear that shit can burn holes in your underwear, if you let it.

Of course, as with all things nasty and inconvenient, there is a "medical" reason for discharge: I'm told it softens the membranes so your vagina can stretch and let the baby through later on. Same reason your nose might be stuffy all the time. Not the baby delivery part, of course. But your nose is a membrane, so it's creating its own discharge for no purpose at all. Mind you, this could be totally wrong. I'm not a doctor. It's just what I picked up here and there.

Take it from me: The "Niagara" flows at its best in the first trimester and last, at least that's how it went for me. That is, you only get a very short break in the middle. So, make sure you pick up some panty liners to pick up the snail trail. You'll save those undies (Granny though they may be . . . see page 23).

Psycho Chick

(Hormonal Rage)

If I had been offered a movie role when I was pregnant, I could've played an amazing Psycho Chick. The first trimester is when Jenny "cuckoo in the head" first showed up for work. And she honestly scared the crap out of my husband. He thought he had lost me forever. And I thought I'd lost myself. The thing is, you know what you're saying is crazy. You are very aware that you're screaming and the veins in your face are pulsating, and it's all over something as stupid as running out of mayonnaise. But knowing that you're being crazy and doing anything to stop yourself are two very different things.

Case in point: One particular evening I was sitting on the couch enjoying a warm cup of tea. My husband decided to join me in my tea drinking. (We almost sound like an English yuppie couple having a cup of tea. We are so not. We had probably just run out of cherry Kool-Aid.) Anyway, he walked into the kitchen and began to read the tea box. He proceeded to tell me, in an alarming manner, that the tea I was drinking was LOADED with caffeine. Well, I'm sure you've all read how caffeine is bad for pregnant women, and I had, too, so I started freaking out. He continued to tell me how much caffeine the tea had. I told him to shut up because I didn't want to hear it. To wind me up, he started shouting that the tea had more caffeine than any other tea in the world. I closed my ears and started screaming for him to shut up. He saw that I had steam coming out of my nose and he was clearly getting a kick out of it. He continued to taunt me, and "Psycho Chick" simply emerged. My face turned beet red, veins popped out, my teeth started grinding, and my eyes crossed: "STOP TELLING ME HOW MUCH FUCKING CAFFEINE I JUST DRANK, I'M ALREADY AFRAID I JUST KILLED THE BABY."

So, guess what my darling, understanding husband did? He kept on going. So, guess what Psycho Chick did? She went positively postal and started whipping remote controls at him. First, the TV control; that one breaks. Then the VCR remote; that one breaks. Then the stereo remote. Now, please listen to me when I tell you this is not me. Not all celebrities are temperamental wack jobs. I am not that kind of a person. I've never thrown anything. But all of a sudden I'm Joan Crawford with a really bad bleach job!

Psycho Chick turned into Crying Psycho Chick, and I burst into tears. My husband realized that he'd played with me long enough and put his arm around me. Psycho Chick went back into her hole that day, but she would be heard from many a time again. Sometimes I'd see her coming, I'd feel her emerging. Other times she would just pop out of the woodwork without warning. But she was always with me, just waiting to make a scene.

Now you might be thinking, "Why did you tell us a story as simple as arguing about the caffeine in tea?" Well, that's exactly why. During this time you will find yourself getting enraged about the dumbest things. They might not seem dumb to you at the time, but they really are, and you'll see the stupidity in retrospect. If you haven't gotten to this point yet in pregnancy, warn your husband that "Psycho Chick" could be coming. At least then when you throw a remote at him, you can say, "I warned you darling . . . now RUN!"

Holy Shit, I Think I Hard-Boiled My Baby!

(Taking Hot Baths)

When you first become pregnant there are so many things you just don't know. Then, there are a billion things people tell you that are either completely wrong or old wives' tales. Then, there's the shit your doctor tells you, and then, there's the shit you read about, and finally, there's the brilliant wisdom your mother feels the need to share.

The day I found out I was pregnant I was so excited that I vowed to change my way of life. Don't get me wrong—I wasn't into anything illegal: I just had some bad eating habits and I was pretty tightly wound. So, I just wanted to eat healthy and really relax. As a start, I thought I would take a hot tub . . . perhaps a Jacuzzi.

I was staying in a hotel at the time, so I figured I would take them up on their advertised facilities. I climbed on into the Jacuzzi and sat there soothing myself in scalding 110-degree water. Oohh, it felt good. As I relaxed, I daydreamed about what my baby would look like. I wondered if he or she would be blond like my husband and me or maybe get my nose and his chin. I was starting to really relax and enjoy myself when Mrs. "I'm Gonna Scare the Shit out of You" decided to join me in the hot tub. She was about fifty years old and, as I came to find out, had three kids of her own. I myself had just found out I was pregnant and I needed to tell somebody, and since she had absolutely no idea who I was, I figured it would be a safe bet to tell her. Of course, I should never have opened my big fat mouth.

"YOU'RE PREGNANT?!! GET THE HELL OUT OF THIS HOT TUB. YOU'RE HURTING YOUR BABY!!!!" she shrieked.

With that, I flip-flopped out of the hot tub like I was in a Jackie Chan movie. I stood there in horror as the once soothing but now terrifyingly lethal water dripped off me. She went on to tell me that extreme heat could really harm the baby, that if your body temperature gets too warm it heats up the embryo.

Now cold and in a cold sweat, I couldn't help but see my new little embryo sitting inside me as a hard-boiled egg. I honestly believed I had hard-boiled my baby. I started freaking out.

Mrs. I'm Gonna Scare the Shit out of You continued her lecture. She told me to avoid taking a bath, and when I showered, it should always be in cool water. Then she went on to tell me that I should avoid eating fish, not to have sex, not to dye my hair, to avoid caffeine, yadadada. I was doing my best to tune her out: She was starting to sound more and more like the teacher in a Charlie Brown cartoon, "Wawawa-waawawa."

All I could think about was that I MIGHT HAVE HARD-BOILED MY BABY! Leaving the still-ranting hot-tubber far behind to call my gyno two time zones away, I ran up to my hotel room and dialed like a mad woman. He assured me that I had NOT, in fact, hard-boiled my baby. However, he did say I should indeed avoid taking hot baths. He also told me that most of the time my body would let me know when it was too hot because when you're pregnant your body will become overheated quickly. And that turned out to be true in a lot of cases. Your body definitely lets you know when something is just not right. If you're in a crowded room that might be too stuffy, your little pregnant body will set off an alarm inside that will make you get the hell out of there.

Now, maybe he had told me all of this before. Maybe the pregnancy books I had read when we were "trying" made all this clear. But in all my happiness and hormonal wackiness, I didn't take any of it in. I guess the lesson here is that you should listen to your body more than you listen to the crazy strangers whose advice will scare your pants off. That is, don't listen to *them*, but do listen to me. Psycho Chick notwithstanding, I'm not crazy even if I am a stranger (about whose privates you already know too much).

Granny Panties
(Letting Go of the G-String)

The moment I got pregnant I swore I would not do typical pregnant things like wear granny panties or a big ugly maternity bra. I was determined that I was going to be different and cool and be a sexy pregnant lady. I suffered and stood my ground for the first few months. I was not giving up my G-string. I loved the no-panty-line look, but as my ass started to widen, my thongs were getting tighter and tighter. Of course I still had no panty line, but instead I had the "your ass is too fat to be wearing those" look going. I had rolls hanging off each side of my hips. Clearly, I had to do something.

So that's how I came to be standing in a store looking at new panty options. Not the maternity store yet. I would give in to that level of sizing a little later in my pregnancy. At this point it was just a regular department store, and I had brought my husband with me for moral support. As I searched the rack he whispered, "Honey, don't shop for my sake; get something comfortable." How sweet, how selfless. So what did I do? I smiled and moved right toward the table of big, wide 100 percent cotton Granny panties. I picked the cutest colors I could find in a couple of sizes (but why are these things only available in white, peach, and baby blue?) and walked in scared slow motion toward the dressing room. I was scared for two reasons. One, I was about to see what size I was going to fit in, and two, the scariest reason, I was about to see my ass in the most unforgiving lighting of all: overhead fluorescent.

I immediately started with the larges. Why not? It would so much easier to go down in size than go through the depressing motion of moving up. On they went, right over my stretched-to-the-limit thong. And surprise, surprise: The large fit. And to my amazement, I had never been so comfortable in my life. Spread the news! Granny panties totally rock! Sexy in the traditional sense, no way. But my newfound comfort seemed like the sexiest thing ever. And there may just be no going back!

To avoid my other fear, and for your information, I avoided looking at my ass altogether. Indeed, and I really believe this, there is absolutely no reason any woman, pregnant or not, should have to look at her naked ass in a department store dressing room. Save that moment for the comfort of your own home and the mirror you bought because it makes you look skinny.

I Can Either Pee on You or You Can Get the Hell Out of My Way!

(Frequent Pee Breaks)

It ought to be something they teach in kindergarten: Do NOT stop a pregnant woman on her way to the bathroom. Unfortunately, even if people understand pregnant pee pressure *in theory,* no one will really understand unless they've been pregnant. The only thing I could tell my husband in order for him to understand my urgency was for him to pretend he had to pee really bad with a refrigerator on top of his bladder. Then I'd ask him to imagine how long HE could hold it!

The weird thing about the pee thing is that it starts almost the moment you find out you're pregnant. That seems so weird to me because there clearly isn't a seven-pound baby pushing on your bladder at that time. Still, I woke up in those early months at 2 a.m. and then at 3 a.m. and then at 6 a.m. No rest for the weary. It was just pee, pee, pee.

Later in my pregnancy, an unusually memorable pee attack happened to me while my husband and I were going to take a drive to visit a friend. He knew it was going to be a bit of a haul, so he asked his very pregnant wife if she had to pee before we left. Well, I didn't at that time, but as we started driving, I felt a small pee sensation. I knew if I said anything he would do the "I told you to pee before we left" routine. So I told myself to save the argument, shut up, and hold it. You know how long I held it for? About fifteen seconds. And therein lies the truth of the matter: There is no "holding it" when you're pregnant. When you gotta go you gotta go!!!

And that's what I told him. But we were almost there, so he "encouraged" me to "hold back the waters." I told him that the only chance I had was for him to drive faster. Zoom! He put the pedal to the metal, but still, I wasn't sure I could hold off and stared longingly out the window at every possible bathroom stop. Greasy gas station bathrooms never looked so good to me.

We turned down the final road to our friends' house. Yes, we were almost there! But then, out of the blue, my husband decided to turn into a freakin' tour guide. He slowed the car down to a snail's pace and started pointing at some stupid well sitting on top of a hill and began to recite the history of the well. Where did Mr. Understanding go? Had he forgotten that the upholstery was in grave danger here? My mouth was to the floor of the car as I held my crotch doing a pee dance. I couldn't believe what he was doing. He obviously did not fully grasp the urgency in my voice. Needless to say, Psycho Chick (remember her?) showed up (see page 15) and I told him where he could shove that well.

Proving that he had not learned that all-important kindergarten lesson, he got upset because I was being mean and he ... completely stopped the car. So you know what I did? I lost my patience (my dignity having been lost years before). I got out of the car, stood on the side of the road, and pulled down my pants and peed. Now, *there's* a pretty picture: a nine months' pregnant lady squatting down trying to balance herself while she pees on the side of the road. Pretty or not, it felt DAMN good.

Moral of the story: When you are in desperate need, don't be afraid to take matters into your own hands. Everyone eventually forgives the pregnant lady.

Passing Stonehenge

(Constipation)

At no time is constipation pretty or comfortable, but during pregnancy it's even worse than bad. And I had it bad. You'll probably notice it most in your first and last trimesters (again, just a small window of relief during that respite known as the second trimester). For me, the worst of it came (or didn't come, to be more precise) in the beginning. I honestly went thirteen days without even a rumble. And I was eating enormous amounts of food. Where could it be going? I wasn't packing weight on just yet . . . and it certainly wasn't coming out.

Then one day, as I was driving my car, BAM! There was no way around it, things were rumbling and they wanted to come out. From the feel of things, I could tell that it was the size of Stonehenge and it was ready to flow. Holy shit! I was thinking, where the hell am I going to go? Even though later on in my pregnancy I wouldn't turn my nose up at a gas station, this was early on, and I refused to use that kind of can. I stepped on the gas and got my eager rectum home.

As I ran to the bathroom, I have to admit that I felt a bit excited. I was finally about to get some relief! Yippee! How could I have known how wrong I'd be? I thought I was giving birth right then and there. The pain! The pushing! You've got to be kidding! My sister was at my house at the time and kept making comments about some banging noise. She kept shouting, "What the hell is that?" It was me, banging my fists against the wall, which were soon followed by my head and feet banging the sink and the tub. Needless to say, things found their way out eventually, but not without great effort and lots of prayers.

And this was only the beginning. It kept happening. Two weeks of nothing and then all of a sudden I'd be on the front line of World War III. I read in books that this was very "normal." Well, screw that. It couldn't be normal. I needed a specialist. So, I dared to ask my gyno for some help, and he referred me to Dr. "I Love Everything about the Butt Canal." Do you think you know where this is going? If you've had a similar experience, I would be very surprised.

As I sat in the waiting room, I couldn't stop think-ing, "Is he gonna look up my butt?" But then I laughed because as I reminded myself, I wasn't there for an exam. I didn't have a colon problem. I was just a preg-nant lady who was really constipated. I just needed a safe laxative. Why my gyno couldn't have prescribed me something I still don't know.

The assistant walked out shouting, "Jenny McCarthy, you're next!" Of course everyone in the waiting room looked up in surprise, and I knew what they were thinking: "Wow, Jenny McCarthy has butt hole prob-lems?" I was so embarrassed, until I realized that they had no right to be smirking: Those assholes were also there because of their own assholes. I felt better already.

I followed the assistant down the hall to the doc-tor's office and met the pro. We talked for thirty min-utes about my butt. Fascinating conversation. The his-tory of it and of my previous ability to crap regularly and yadda yadda. Then, he casually asked if I partook in anal sex. I don't care if he's a doctor or not, it was just a really weird thing for me to hear. Of course I made a vulgar face and, clearly offended, I said, "NO!" He didn't sense my outrage.

He continued on about how butt sex can be very bad for your butt. I'm like, dude, I'm just a pregnant lady; shut the hell up and help me. Finally, he started to fill me in on my safe options. "Drink more water and eat better," he said. Well, no, shit, Sherlock! As he wrapped things up, I took my car keys out of my purse to show him I was ready to GO. He stood up and gestured to walk me out. I couldn't help but think, "Thank God! I'm outta this loony place."

We walked down the hallway and he had one of his hands on my shoulder. No biggie. Just being nice. Well, his hand on my shoulder turned into more of a steering wheel. And he steered me right into an examination room. Okay, at this point I looked like a deer caught in the headlights because we all know what was about to happen.

He told me to undress and put a gown on, and he shut the door to give me some privacy. Why privacy is a concern in that line of work, I don't know! Of course I was freaking out. I kept thinking, "Should I run?" or "Should I just tough it out?" I figured that my gyno had sent me here, and I trusted his judgment. I took my clothes off and decided to take it like a man, so to speak.

The good doctor came back into the room and had me lie on my side with my bare ass hanging out toward him. He told me he was going to slide a tool inside my bum and remove a piece of stool. You think you're surprised to read this? I was thinking, "YOU'VE GOT TO BE KIDDING! NO FREAKIN' WAY!" But he lubed up and wazam . . . what's up, Doc? But just when I thought it couldn't get worse, it did.

You'll probably scream, but I have to tell you because I couldn't believe it myself. This specialist, this "I Love Everything about the Butt Canal" guy, proved his love of the job: He pulled the tool out with the poo-poo connected to it and sniffed it! No shit; pun intended. He totally sniffed it. He said, "I'm going to smell it now," and boy, did he. I don't know the medical reason behind the need to smell the ol' stool. Maybe there isn't one. Maybe he really loves his job, if you know what I mean. I should have asked my gyno about all this, but once I got the hell out of there, I never looked back. And I never went back.

Instead, I took to heart what everyone had been telling me from the start: Constipation during pregnancy is normal. It isn't pretty, it isn't comfortable, and it sure doesn't smell good. But relief will come. If not every few weeks, then after delivery! So just hang in there and stay far away from specialists. Constipation is normal in pregnancy, even if it feels like you're passing Stonehenge!

Is It a Penis or a Vagina?

(Finding Out the Sex)

I'm one of those people who believes if you can find out something, you FIND OUT. Screw surprises. If I could've found out what this baby's occupation was going to be, I would have. Speaking for my need-to-know self here, I simply felt that if I knew what the sex was I would be able to bond even more with my baby.

That said, I didn't have a firm grip on my preference. I kept bouncing from wanting a little girl to wanting a little boy. My wanting a little girl was for obvious reasons: someone to get my nails done with, to teach some cheerleading moves to, to pass down my jewelry and my Gucci dresses to. But then I would really want a boy, some little tough tyke who I could wrestle around with and who would be my little man. Of course my husband wanted a boy first. He loved the idea of having a mini version of himself running around in this world. But either way, it goes without saying that we both would have been ecstatic with a girl or a boy. Good thing, too. Chances are that we were going to get one or the other!

Most people find out the sex of their baby (if they choose to) through ultrasound at about twenty weeks, but you can find out earlier and more accurately if you decide to have some genetic tests done earlier. For one, there is a test called CVS, which is short for chorionic villus sampling. Sounds bad but it's ultimately good: It tests whether or not your baby has Down syndrome. It's usually performed between nine and eleven weeks, and you find out the results within a week. Joy of joys, they perform this test by going up your wazoo and having a needle pluck through your uterus to gain some fluid for testing.

Another test is called amniocentesis. This is usually performed at sixteen weeks. Instead of going up your wazoo, the needle is poked through your lower belly to extract fluid. With amniocentesis, it takes longer to find out the results because they count the chromosomes to make sure Junior has no abnormalities. Both tests are considered invasive, but if you're thirty-five or over, the doc usually wants you to have one of these tests done because your chance of having a child with Down syndrome increases each year. So remember, not only do WE get old and ugly, our eggs do, too.

I opted for amniocentesis. I was under the thirty-five age marker but I still wanted it done. I wanted to know that my baby was healthy so I could relax throughout the rest of my pregnancy. Even though I hoped for relaxation on the horizon, I was nervous because of how big that damn needle looked on all those pregnancy shows I had seen. Sorry to have to break it to you, but in reality . . . it's still damn big.

In preparation for sticking the needle in my belly, the doc looked around with the ultrasound. A woman this time, she checked to see if there was enough fluid for the baby to float around in and then began to check his or her extremities so that she wouldn't poke one with the needle. My husband and I laughed as we looked at the little toes and fingers. Then the doctor told us that we might be able to tell what the sex was right then, just by looking on the ultrasound screen. She said she couldn't be absolutely certain until the results of the amnio came back, but she said from what she could see, it would be a pretty good guess. So, of course we asked her to go for it, to go ahead and make an educated guess. As she moved the ultrasound camera down my belly, my husband and I held hands and smiled. We were holding our breath out of pure excitement. She stopped the camera on a certain spot, and without saying a word, my husband smiled so big it could have ripped his face apart. His eyes lit up as he shouted, "That's a penis . . . YES!" Low and behold, he was right. There was the largest baby penis on that screen that I have ever seen (not that I've seen all that many, mind you). Even the doc looked a little surprised. She nodded at my husband and told him that it looked pretty good that we had ourselves a boy.

A BOY!! I was so excited that my eyes filled with tears. I was having a little boy. YEAH!! But my little bubble of happiness was burst wide open when she told me she was preparing the needle. Uh-oh. Now I was scared again. I closed my eyes and tried to relax. I started envisioning me and my little baby boy playing on a beach. I saw his little smile as I threw him up in the air and heard his little giggles. By keeping my focus on my vision the procedure came and went. The needle going in sounded a little like piercing the skin on a nicely cooked Thanksgiving turkey, but it didn't hurt at all. I opened my eyes, smiled, and looked at my husband. He was greener than a Martian. I guess watching something like that can't be too good for the hubby. Of course, months later, at delivery time, he would get his fill of gory sights!

A few weeks after the amnio, my gyno left a message on our machine that ours was a healthy baby and that we were right . . . the penis we'd seen was definitely a penis. A little boy was headed our way!

I have to imagine that the joy of finding out your child's gender would be just as powerful if you were to find out after all the pushing and grunting of delivery. But to this day, the memory of the moment we found out is deeply etched in my mind, and imagining him as a him for months thereafter was a luxury I wouldn't have traded for the world.

Can I Have a Mustard Sandwich with Pickles, Anchovies, Peanut Butter, and a Little Cottage Cheese? . . . Oh, and Throw a Few Fish Sticks on There!

(Cravings)

Why do we women have such unusual cravings during pregnancy? Food cravings, that is. No doubt our men crave other things, but this book is limited to the female experience!

I used to think that our bodies knew what nutrients we needed and would crave that particular food. Could that be true? The experts say so, but I don't know.

Could there really be redeeming nutrients in some of the things we pregnant gals simply *must have*?

All I know is that some of my cravings were doozies! And I had them really early on. Indeed, my cravings were one of the first signs that I was knocked up, before I officially knew. I woke up one morning and rolled over and told my husband that I wanted to squirt a bottle full of mustard in my mouth. Now, what's important to understand here is that I hate mustard! My whole life I have despised the yellow mushy stuff. Until that morning, of course, when I wanted it so badly that I could have bathed in it.

My husband looked at me like I was nuts, and then he began to smirk. He sat up in bed and shouted that I was SOOO pregnant. I laughed and thought he had lost his marbles. There wasn't a tiny bit of hesitation about this. At that time (this is pre–dipstick in New Orleans), I honestly still believed I wasn't pregnant. My husband teased me for days about this. I was so sure the mustard thing was a fluke, I bet my husband forty million dollars that I wasn't pregnant. (No, I don't have forty million dollars. It's just a stupid thing my husband and I do for fun . . . by the way, even though I lost this one, he's in the hole eighty million.)

Later in the game, what really got my cravings all fired up were food commercials (the weeks of being nauseated clearly behind me). I would be plopped on the couch with my feet up like a good pregnant lady and bam . . . on the TV was the most delicious product I'd ever seen. In fact, it seemed to me to be the best Shake 'N' Bake commercial ever made. I still can't believe how good they made that chicken look. And they proved that it was easy! Shit, I had to get me some Shake 'N' Bake right then and there. So, I went waddling off to the store. And this kind of thing happened almost daily. I would tune into commercials just to see what rang my bell, and that's what I would go hunt down or make my husband go hunt down. I have to say, he was SO great when it came to this. If he had to drive forty minutes for a dozen Krispy Kremes at midnight, he would and did. (For the reason why, recall his brush with Psycho Chick.)

Succulent, juicy TV chicken aside, my cravings were also triggered by the mere mention of some kinds of food. For instance, if someone innocently mentioned to me how great the steak was at a new restaurant, I needed a reservation STAT! And here's where celebrity comes in handy . . . guess what pregnant lady was sittin' her fat ass there that night? Abuse of power, perhaps, but I just couldn't help myself.

Not necessarily a doozy of a craving by content standards, my incredible need for homemade brownies must have set a volume record. Toward the last few months of pregnancy, my need for them was rapidly increasing. In the last month I made them every night and ate them ALL in one sitting . . . every night! No joke. No exaggeration.

There's no doubt that eating food felt so great after having been sick at the sight of most foods earlier on. But to this day, I simply can't believe the orgasmic effect you can get from surrendering to your cravings. Since you don't really get a whole lot of action in the bedroom (see page 147 for more on that), I advise all pregnant women to surrender to these cravings and get off by indulging in your favorite foods. Remember, you've finally got one of the best excuses in the world to pig out. Do what I did and enjoy every stinkin' moment of it. If you're just dying for a sardine sandwich with whipped cream, go for it, sister; it's soooo worth it!

Where in the Hell Can I Find a Muumuu?

(Nothing to Wear)

———————————

Clothes shopping when you're feeling even a little bloated is tough on the self-esteem, if not on the wallet. Still, I've been pretty lucky, and with a stylist's help (just one of those celeb perks!), I've never had too much trouble finding clothes that make me look good. That all changed when I first started to show. Actually, and you probably know how this goes, I was likely the only one who thought I was showing. I was just growing what I now refer to as "a protective fat layer" around my belly. To me it was obvious I was pregnant but to the rest of the world Jenny McCarthy was simply eating too many Krispy Kremes.

One day I looked in my closet to put something on to start my day. I threw on a pair of pants only to realize that I couldn't quite button them. I got the zipper up but that damn button just wouldn't close. I thought to myself, well, this totally sucks. So I took them off and tried on all of my other pants until I found a pair that were always a little big on me. Except this time they just fit. I put on a nice fitted top only to look in the mirror and see that "protective fat layer" around my belly. So I proceeded to try on every other top I had until I found the loosest fitting one. I ended up with a massive pile of clothes on my closet floor and an outdated baggy look for the day. Ugh.

Finding something to wear will only get worse before it gets better, so here's my advice to you: Stretch this part out as long as you can and cram yourself into your regular loose-fitting clothes. You're in that awful stage where you don't yet look pregnant, just fat. No stylist in the world can really help you hide this. All of the pregnancy books will tell you to throw on one of your husband's shirts. Not terrible advice, but at this "fat" stage, I don't know about you, but I don't look that cute in a flannel!

Don't go out and buy maternity clothes yet. With the exception of some basic black stretch pants, maternity clothes are made for women with bellies. Or for women who have told the world they are expecting to get one. Early on, you honestly won't fit in them, and you'll look like a jackass with all that extra floppy fabric.

Of course, I thought I had it worse than anybody. Because of my work, I had to hide my pregnancy. Squeezing into my clothes and hiding my fat was freakin' impossible. And okay, maybe this particular brand of impossible won't happen to you, but national TV spot aside, you're going to be able to relate to the theme of this next story.

Dick Clark asked me to host the American Music Awards, and by the time I would have to do the show, I would already be a few months pregnant. Terrified to have my cover blown but excited about the job, I agreed.

Poor little rich girl, I know, but my wardrobe stylist and I went through a horrific disaster in trying to help me dress cool but all the while hide my belly. Prepregnancy, I usually wore a size 4 or 6, but now I was only barely squeezing into a size 12. We had at least ten "try-on" sessions, which all ended in tears. I would seriously break down and bawl. All of my pre-interviews were about what I was going to wear (ah, Hollywood priorities!). For the first time I heard myself dissing style. "Who cares about clothes?" I said. "It's about being funny." Yeah, right, not to Dolce & Gabbana.

Fast-forward to show time and I was about to go out onstage. I was feeling confident because no one had said anything to me about my weight gain. I was uncomfortable as hell, though, because I was wearing a corset so tight I couldn't breathe. (Of course, I asked my doctor about wearing one at least a million times: "Am I hurting the baby?" No, he told me. "Am I smashing the baby?" No, he said. "Am I killing the baby?" "NO! You're only hurting yourself. He's not going to be in pain. You are!" "Well, okay then, as long as I'm the only one suffering I'm happy.")

The moment of truth: "Ladies and Gentlemen, here are your hosts Sean 'P. Diddy' Combs and Jenny McCarthy." I walked out onstage feeling good, feeling fine, connected with my mojo. Some people made faces at my weird clothing choices (Did I mention the corset?), but I didn't care as long as the world didn't think I looked pregnant.

Several hours later (I know, these shows really do go on!) and, to my relief, the end of the show finally arrived. I plopped down on the couch in my dressing room and welcomed my family, who had been sitting in the audience. "How did I do?" They all smiled and clapped and said I did really well except . . . "Except what?" I asked. My sister began to tell me how the people all around them had been commenting on how pregnant I looked. I guess it's true: You just can't keep a secret in Hollywood.

Again, this might not happen to you, but national airwaves aside again, you may have had a nightmare experience along these lines. The next day Howard Stern went on the air and made comments about how pregnant I looked. He said I had pregnant boobs. Coming from him, I *think* that's a compliment, but it's not exactly what a girl wants to hear.

First-trimester flab behind me (and on my behind), my next month was fun. I was obviously pregnant, the world knew it, and I could finally shop for maternity clothes. What I didn't know was how awful some maternity clothes can be. They have gotten better, I think, but not good enough. First of all, they are so overpriced. But you're kind of screwed—What choice do you have?—so you have to buy some. You have nothing else. Here's what I know: The key to shopping at this point is comfort. I bought comfy tanks and draw-string pants and cozy turtlenecks. I wore them almost every day until my ninth month, when I porked out beyond belief. I refused to go buy still more and still larger and expensive maternity clothes to wear for just a few more weeks, so I begged my husband to go to Sears and get me a damn muumuu! I'm not kidding. I would beg anyone that heard my cry to go get me a muumuu. Nothing fit me right, and if it did, I just looked so incredibly large or I was really uncomfortable. I wanted a muumuu, just like the ones Mrs. Roper wore on *Three's Company*.

Then it happened! One of my friends heard my call. Behold the muumuu. She held up a giant, blue-flowered muumuu, and it had my name written all over it. I put it on and danced all around the house. My glory ended as soon as my husband saw me in it and begged me to take it off (not to get some action, believe me. Even the friend who bought it for me said it was just "wrong." I say, "Bite me!"

If you get to that point where you just can't take it, please go get one. MUUMUU'S really do rock!

Freddy Krueger
Ain't Got Nothing on Me!

(Dreams)

I've always been one to have wild dreams, but no one told me how bizarre they could be when you're pregnant. Throughout my life I've always written down my dreams and looked their meaning up in my dream dictionary. Well, by golly, they don't really have anything that falls under giving birth to a green slimy cocoon that wiggles and flies away. Desperate to find deeper meaning, I looked up *green,* but I'm pretty sure that "having great pleasure with simple things" doesn't really apply. So far, this pregnancy had not been especially pleasant, nor had it been simple!

Wacked-out green dreams aside, I had one recurring dream while pregnant that I still get a kick out of. To this day, when I think back I smile. And dream dictionary definition or not, it's clear to me that it was a dream about looking forward to motherhood. It's going to sound weird at first, like all dreams do, so just hang in there with me. Here goes.

I would dream of lying in bed sleeping or resting. Feeling a bit lonely and sad, I would grab a medical tool (which resembled a razor blade and just happened to be nearby) and perform my own C-section. I would pull my baby out and play with him right there in the bed. We would talk and giggle and I would hug and squeeze him. As soon as I would start to feel like this couldn't possibly be good for him, I would put him back in my belly and sew myself up. I had this dream and performed this delicate operation throughout my pregnancy. Sometimes my baby had no nose or ears and I would sort of freak out, but for the most part I would look forward to the dream. I felt like I was getting to know my son before he even came out into the world.

One time I dreamed of him as an older child . . . like seven years old. I dreamed he came running in the bedroom while I was sleeping and put his little head on the edge of my bed and nudged me. I remember looking at him and smiling, thinking how cute he was and how he looked nothing like me. He was an exact seven-year-old replica of my husband. This always made me wonder: If you dream of a specific face, is that actually what your child will look like? And then I wondered, if the answer is yes, then what about the dreams where I delivered a green slimy cocoon? Who knows? Maybe I am a psychic and was foreseeing all those diaper changes!

Since I'm sharing, let me tell you that the best pregnant dreams are your sex dreams. In mine, when I remembered the details, I was pregnant and gorgeous—all airbrushed like Demi Moore on the cover of *Vanity Fair*. But even when I didn't remember the specifics, I'd know I'd had one because I'd wake up in the middle of an orgasm! How's that for outstanding? Believe me, this does happen, and quite frankly I wish it happened more often. Here's hoping you get to experience it!

In the meantime, keep a journal of your dreams. You'll definitely get a kick out of them when you go back and read about them later on.

Is That an Apple on Your Rectum, or Are You Just Happy to See Me?

(Hemorrhoids)

I'd seen the Preparation H commercials and I'd laughed my share of laughs at the actor's discomfort, but now I realize that hemorrhoids are no laughing matter. These little devils can show up during pregnancy or, as with me, after delivery. When and if they rear their ugly heads in your rear, know that you're not alone and that your doctor has seen them before. Yes, he has. Even ones as big as yours (we all think we've set records, honey, so get over it!).

Given that I'd made it through almost my entire pregnancy without a hemmie, and considering the fact that my little constipation problem (Stonehenge any-one?) had me pushing hard enough to bring them out if they were ever planning on coming out, I thought for sure I was home free. But there was no escaping them. Out they came and out they wanted to stay.

If you've never had hemorrhoids before, you're going to be shocked when you peer around at your ass with a mirror and see the bloated balloon knot that greets you there. See yours for yourself, but let me be the one who describes how they feel.

When you've got a hemorrhoid and you go "Number Two," you're likely going to get a feeling down there like a sharp pinch. As the poopie comes out, you will think you are passing peanuts. Then as the poo progresses down, you will also think you are passing peanut shells. So I avoided going Number Two until I became so constipated that I was forced to go to the hospital. After I moaned in the emergency room for seven hours, the doctors came to a conclusion: I'm full of shit. I told them about my hemorrhoids, and they prescribed a stool softener.

If you are unfortunate enough to experience these painful little buggers, ask your doc for some stool softeners (but remember not to go to a specialist unless you absolutely have to). It will make those peanuts feel more like peanut butter. Wow—I can't believe I just said that!

Hi, Porn Star!

(Engorged Breasts)

––––––––––––––––––––––––––

If you've never had breasts before (as in boobs that need a bra), or even if you've already got quite a rack, watch out and get ready, because whoppers are on their way!

You probably noticed that your breasts became very sore the moment you found out you were pregnant. It's true what the books say: The soreness will eventually go away. But be forewarned: The sprawling balloons where your manageable boobs used to be will continue to enlarge.

My breasts became so out-of-control huge and heavy that I actually weighed them. I have a food scale, and I just had to know how they'd compare to a meal, so I plopped a breast up on the little metal tray. Each breast: five pounds. That's ten pounds of breast. Think of that in terms of chicken and you'll quickly see that your breasts could feed a family of eight or ten people! Though there are guys in this world who might disagree, to me that's totally insane! I guess the bright side is that I would rather have ten pounds go to my chest than to my ass.

Not only did my boobs get enormous, but they got that way very quickly. By the end of the second month of pregnancy, I was already out buying new bras. I needed major support to hold up these new bowling balls. But I refused to buy a maternity bra because they looked like they were for Grandma's big boobs (it wasn't until a little later that I gave in and went for coverage of Granny's big ass; recall page 23). So I went to the department store and tried on a 36D. Unfortunately, at that size, they ALL look like Grandma bras. Without an option, I bit the bullet, bought my big ugly bras, and wore them day and night. Yes, I said night, too. I noticed that wearing them when I slept really kept my boobs from sliding around and hanging off the sides of the mattress.

A few months later I was once again shocked as I attempted to put my big, ugly bra on one morning. And it wouldn't fit. My boobs were at it again. Unbelievable. I just couldn't believe my eyes. And then I noticed that not only had my boobs grown but my areolas had turned into National Geographic nipples. (You know,

those Ubangi tribe women with nipples as big as dinner plates.) And to top it all off they had turned dark
brown. Prepregnancy, my areolas were cute, small, and
pink. Now they looked like burned pancakes. I was
freakin'.

I didn't care if my husband was having fun with my
new giant boobs. I wasn't going to let him get a look
at this. I was totally embarrassed. As far as I was con-
cerned, what I had for him to play with weren't play-
worthy anymore. I needed help. So where does one go
to get understanding, camaraderie, and answers? Well,
there's this book for you. But for me, it was off to the
maternity store.

For a place I had wanted no part of, I don't think I
could have run there fast enough. This was my new
home, a place where other women walked around
with giant brown nipples, too. And there, standing
before me, was a giant rack of the ugliest, biggest, and
most comfortable-looking bras I had ever seen. A
MATERNITY BRA! I just had to try that bitch on so fast
that I didn't even bother to close the dressing room
door. Ah, comfort beyond belief. Take it from me and
don't hold out for style. Don't wait long to join the
team. Surrender to the maternity bra and your world
will be transformed.

If I scared you at all about how big your boobs are
going to get while pregnant, then you're in deep shit

because compared to milk-filled boobs, you ain't seen nothin' yet!!

When your milk comes in, you and Pamela Anderson can share bras. True enough. There aren't enough words that can accurately describe what happens. "Hi, Porn Star!" is just the beginning.

Here's how it goes down: As if your body hasn't been through enough already, a few days after delivery, your breasts are going to start getting sore. When I told my mom that mine were sore, I saw a little panic in her eyes. She obviously knew what I was about to go through. I kept reassuring her it was all okay. I'd been through the worst of it with breast surgery before, and I really thought I could "do" boob pain.

Fast forward to . . . (crying) "MOM, I NEED HELP! I can't take the pain, I'm either going to die or cut off my breasts." It's crazy how badly they hurt, and I was already on painkillers so I couldn't even imagine what they would feel like sober. When I tell you that I walked over to the mirror and lifted my shirt and sobbed ridiculously, you have to believe me. Now for all those breast feeders out there, I hear that feeding your baby can immediately relieve this pain and engorgement. But they will engorge uncomfortably before each feeding until you're into a routine. I was not breast feeding, so I had to fight it and let them dry up. They were so swollen that the top part of my boobs were hitting my collarbone and the bottom half touched my belly button (only a slight exaggeration, I promise you).

If, like me, you aren't going to breast-feed, you're going to go through the wringer like me, too. I don't want to scare you, but in some respects, I have to say that this boob thing was more baffling to me than delivery. It all happens so fast (the engorgement, that is, not the relief) and there's not much you can do.

Some people told me to ice my mams, but the only thing I could find that would fit were two huge bags of frozen vegetables (we're talking commercial-sized bags, here), and they melted too quickly. Another person suggested I wrap my boobs in cabbage leaves. I don't know about you, but even if this old wives' tale really works, I wasn't up to the challenge. About all I can suggest that I know works is to bind your breasts up (think Hillary Swank in *Boys Don't Cry* and Gwyneth Paltrow in *Shakespeare in Love*). I used a long scarf and didn't take it off my chest for days. Just taking it off for a shower was excruciating. Any little movement was agony. So much to look forward to, eh?

Ready and Squeeze . . . Your Kegels

(An Exercise for the Vagina)

Throughout your pregnancy you're going to hear women whining about Kegels. "Are you doing your Kegels?" "Make sure you're doing your Kegels or you'll be sorry." Even women who aren't pregnant are going to warn you to pay attention to your Kegels. I'm not saying don't do them. People swear by them. I was just always so annoyed with them. Who really wants to squeeze her vagina in and out all day long? Woman-to-woman advice aside, where's the scientific proof that Kegels will *really* do any good? I swear I wouldn't have done them if the I've-had-a-baby-and-so-take-it-from-me sisterhood hadn't scared me into squeezing.

So let's say you've been scared or pressured into vagina flexing. How do you know you're doing it right? Obviously, there's no personal trainer to spot you on this one! If you want to know if you're doing your Kegels right, give this a try: The next time you're peeing, stop the flow of urine midstream. The muscles you're using to do this *are* your Kegels and they are the ones you should be trying to flex all day. But more than needing to know why this is important to do, don't you wonder who discovered this magic muscle?

Beyond guessing that it was someone named Kegel, I don't know the answer to the who, only to the why. Kegels are supposed to improve muscle tone in your wazoo so your post-delivery healing process is a lot faster. That is, after you blow out your vagina in delivery these magical Kegels are supposed to help make it bounce back into shape. Strong Kegels are also supposed to help you regain control of your leaky bladder after delivery.

Even though doing my Kegels annoyed me, my husband kept bugging me to do them because he was scared that the next time we had sex it would feel like he was throwing a hot dog down a hallway. And I believe those were his exact words. So, there I was on the couch watching *Friends*, squeezing away. And there I was in a supermarket line uncomfortably doing my Kegels thinking everyone knew that my vagina was squeezing in and out. And there I was on the phone talking to my mom, and she's completely unaware her daughter was doing Kegels. Bizarre.

In the end, I say if it's really possible to get your vagina "back in shape" after delivery, go ahead and do those Kegels. There's nothing worse than a big, sloppy vagina. You want to keep that thing pretty as long as you can!

Well, It's Not 1972 Anymore!

(Baby Boomers Explaining
How It Was in Their Day)

God love the baby boom generation. Boomers are really making getting old look good. They're not going to surrender to a rocking chair. They're going to keep going to their Weight Watchers meetings and doing their cardio class twice a week. And they're clearing the path for our generation to have more respect when we get older. More power to them.

All this said, I have to say that there are just too many baby boomers out there, and all of them seem to have advice about how pregnancy should be "done." Here's an example: My mom's a boomer, and her take on pregnancy weight gain just blows my mind. Back when she was preggers the doctors were extremely strict about gaining weight. And if you ask most of these baby boomers what they gained, they'll tell you about eighteen pounds. And do you want to know the reason why? From my perspective, it's clear that the reason is that all the doctors were men and wanted to keep the chicks skinny. But it's also because back then the average woman was nineteen or twenty when she started having babies. Now, as you know, women are having babies in their late twenties, their late thirties, and even into their forties. We're coming in older and heavier, and we're packing weight in proportion to our age! Good news: The doctors (lots more of them are women now, too!) and books say gaining twenty-five to thirty-five pounds is normal nowadays.

But I've done a little research myself, and I think those books and experts are even a little off. Most women I've talked to gained about fifty pounds. Sure, there are annoying exceptions, but I swear most were in the fifty zone. Even my doctor said fifty was pretty normal. Of course, I surpassed this new normal by ten pounds, but you get what I'm saying. Maybe Mother doesn't always know best, you know?

I remember one day in the gym I was walking on the treadmill and a baby boomer was next to me. She struck up a conversation about my pregnant belly and proceeded to ask me how much weight I'd gained so far. I thought the question took balls, but I didn't mind sharing. At that point (seven months pregnant), I had gained thirty-five pounds. I told her and she almost fell off the treadmill. Her eyes bugged out and she screeched, "YOU'VE GOT TO BE KIDDING! WELL, YOU BETTER SLOW DOWN THERE, SWEETIE, BECAUSE THAT'S JUST RIDICULOUS." I couldn't believe she was going off on me. She continued to explain that back in her day, she only gained eighteen pounds. I couldn't hold back, I shouted at her, "IT'S NOT 1972 ANYMORE!"

Weight gain is one thing. But then there are the "Well back in our day we had no epidural" women. My feeling here is God bless ya, but don't even think for one second we are going to go without just because you did. It's a whole different time; our way of living has dramatically changed. Modern medicine has *advanced things,* ladies. We love hearing the story of your personal ordeal, but please don't lecture or make us feel like we're doing pregnancy wrong just because we're doing it better (uh, I mean different).

Did a Sewer Tank Explode, or Did You Just Fart?

(Gas)

————————————

My poor poor husband. He has always enjoyed the real side of Jenny—after all, he knew something about me before we got together—but I don't think he ever expected this.

Now, we've all eaten something bad and suffered the consequences, especially while driving in a car with the windows rolled up, but a pregnant woman's farts can truly bring a man to his knees. Things start getting bad in the first trimester. Unfortunately, when you don't look pregnant (only fat) you don't get too much sympathy; no one cuts you much slack. But even if you don't look like you have an excuse, you have no control either. You just kind of have to hope that a sweet little smile and an "oops" will get you off the hook.

The worst time for me and my gas was when we were out in public. I would feel the gas building up, and I'd run to an empty aisle in the store and pray no one decided to come along when I released my poison. Another effective but risky strategy is to do the ol' walking while you're farting routine hoping that the stench dissipates as you move. But come on, you know that there will never fail to be some poor bastard who will walk directly into your line of fire.

Obviously, the main reason behind the alluring odor of these precious bursts of air is constipation. If you try to stay away from gassy foods and/or simply not gorge yourself, you might have an easier time than I did. But either way, I highly suggest carrying a little air freshener spray in your purse. And for the home, invest in some scented candles. Your husband might think you're trying to be romantic, so just go with it if you can stand it. Remember, he doesn't need to know that you're trying to cover the smell of death. And if anything escapes accidentally, at least you're trying!

Hands Off, Dude!

(Strangers Touching Your Belly)

─────────────

It would be great if we lived in a world where strangers weren't so strange. In civilized society, people don't just come up to you and touch your stomach. If they did, you might have them arrested! So why do people think it's okay to come up to pregnant women and pet their bellies?

Now, I know most people mean well, but I would imagine that you'll feel as protective of your belly as I did mine. And as a general rule, I think they should all ASK FIRST, don't you agree? I remember a couple of times when I was wearing a tank top that showed a bit of my bare belly, and total strangers (once a completely greasy guy) would think that the exposed skin was okay to touch. No, off limits! Back off. The people who touched me are just lucky that I didn't bite their hands off like a guard dog. Woof! Woof! Stay away.

One particular encounter with an old Jamaican lady gave me the willies on top of making me angry. I was walking down the street and she stopped me, placed her hand on my belly, and began chanting a voodoo-like prayer. I was in such shock that I couldn't move. Maybe it was wandering mind syndrome (see page 95), but before I had time to kung-foo her, she was already gone. I was so freaked out afterward that I got my ass home and scrubbed my belly, saying my own Catholic prayer.

The one exception to my rule of ASK FIRST was when other pregnant women touched my belly. I think you'll agree that there is an unspoken camaraderie between all pregnant women and you want to share the moment every time you see each other. There's that knowing look and smile we give each other as we pass. So I say, if another preggie wants to touch the belly, she can go right ahead. But the door is only open to those of us in the knocked-up club.

I Can't See! I'm Bleeding! I Can't Stand It!

(Weird and Painful Bits and Pieces)

Obviously, this whole book is devoted to all the strange things that happen to you while pregnant. Let me take a minute to horrify you on some of the finer points in the "Did you know?" category.

Did you know that leg cramps can be really frequent, especially in the last trimester? Wake-you-up-in-the-middle-of-the-night-in-a-cold-sweat leg cramps? Leg cramps feel just like growing pains if you can remember back that far, you old fart. For me, about the only thing that helped was to try to walk through them. As in get my fat ass off the couch and walk around a bit. But when they were really bad, I would beg my husband to rub them out when I could stand to have him touch them at all. Note: Have that massage oil standing by.

And are you expecting blurred vision? Brace yourself. Blurred vision does not happen to all pregnant women so don't freak out. But for all of you who wake up and can't see your hand in front of your face, I just want you to know that this IS a side effect of pregnancy. My doctor told me that some women need to get their eyeglass prescription changed during their pregnancy because their vision is radically different. For what it's worth, mine went back to normal after delivery.

Remember what I told you about the snail trail discharge and the likelihood that your nose would play the same game? Yes, it's true: Runny noses usually happen early in the pregnancy and could last the whole damn time. I had sneezing attacks that would go on for hours because of my softening nasal membranes. Wait, it gets better: Bloody noses are also big in pregnancy, so keep that Kleenex box next to your bed.

Speaking of blood, know this: Bleeding gums are not necessarily a sign of gingivitis. Pregnancy can make that toothbrush turn pink. Because nothing about my pregnancy was half-assed, I looked like a vampire that had been sucking someone's neck all night long. Needless to say, I went through a few toothbrushes.

And speaking of veins, the dark line on your belly isn't one. A vein, that is. It's officially called the linea nigra and it's just a line. That's all. Doctors don't seem to know why some women get it and others don't. It doesn't hurt, of course. But I don't think it's terribly attractive! As with all things in this department, there's no way to get rid of the line, but it does go away after you give birth. Fair warning: If you're brave enough to sport a bikini while pregnant, know that exposing your belly to the sun might make the linea nigra darker.

Believe it or not, the one and only symptom or side effect I did *not* have the pleasure of living through myself while pregnant was spider veins. I got everything else, so I have no idea why God stopped here. I did get one varicose vein that I thought was both nasty-looking and seriously uncomfortable, but after hearing my friends talk about their spider veins, I stopped complaining about my little varicose vein and shut my trap.

It turns out (I asked) that spider veins are caused by an increase in estrogen in your system. And I've also heard that people who stand a lot have a better chance of getting them. I asked my girlfriend about them, and she told me that hers started to spin their webs in the fourth month and got progressively worse from there. She said that her beautiful model legs (her description, not mine) started to look like the grandma who got run over by a reindeer. They were puffy, purpley, and squiggly, and she was mortified. She cried at her doctor's office, and he told her she had actually been lucky because he had seen some women with spider veins that looked like grapes hanging off a vine—gnarled and crisscrossed and bulbous. I'm so sorry if you ever get them that bad, but rest assured that they almost always disappear after delivery. My friend's did. She's back to wearing short skirts and heels. See, you, too, will be back skanking it up in no time at all!

www.ihavetostopbuyingbabyshit.com
(On-Line Baby Stores)

———————————

Somebody stop me!!!

There was no doubt about it and even I can admit it: I needed help. My husband tried to find me some rehab, but it turns out that there are no clinics for out-of-control, shopaholic moms-to-be. But hey, if you can't get out of the house, what else is there for you to do? You shop the Web for the cutest, most adorable baby stuff money can buy. I did. You probably will. I won't blame you.

For me, the problem began when I registered for my baby shower. A friend told me to register on-line because it would make it easier for me and for those buying for me. So I found a good store on-line and registered. Once I got there, I saw all these links to other baby stores and nursery stores and specialty stores and so on. So I just thought I would take a look-see at some of them. The next thing I knew we had a stack of boxes outside our door. My husband was fine with my spending at first. It wasn't until the other sixty boxes came that he basically lost a nut. The key to controlling his temper was being smart enough to buy a few "I love my daddy" bibs. I would open up a box and say, "But look how cute, honey; he loves his daddy."

That trick may have calmed him down, but little did he know that from then on, I had stuff delivered to my sister's house. I finally slowed down when I realized I had almost spent our nest egg on crap our baby would probably never really appreciate. A word to the wise: Shopping on the Web is always hard to resist, but when you're pregnant and hormonal and have nothing better to do for the afternoon, shopping on the Web is like entering the Bermuda triangle. It looks fun and relaxing, but you'll never find a way out. Quit while you're ahead and toss the computer in the attic the moment you find out you're in the family way.

Is It Hot in Here or Is It Just Me? . . . It's Just Me

(Hot Flashes and Fainting Spells)

Pregnancy made me sweat. I think that's why they say pregnant women glow. I had a constant layer of sweat on my face. Between the slickness of the sweat and my out-of-control body temperature, you could have fried eggs and bacon right on my forehead.

If you're like me, hot flashes and fainting spells could be some of the first symptoms to let you know that you're pregnant. I remember standing in checkout lines with sweat dripping down my face. And then I'd get dizzy. I'm grateful I don't have any embarrassing fainting stories but every once in a while I would get dizzy enough to plow into walls. (Being blond I could get away with it.) If you're in a stuffy room with no air circulating, you're asking for it.

If you live somewhere with a cool climate, you're one lucky gal. Take it from me: Living in any kind of heat (like Los Angeles) while pregnant can wipe a lady out. I got to the point where, in our house at night, I had the air-conditioning on fifty degrees (in nothing but Granny undies—lots of fabric and plenty of coverage but not lots of warmth) while my husband was forced to wear a parka and mittens. He kept complaining that icicles were forming on his nose. Of course, reasonable and emotionally balanced pregnant woman that I was, I didn't care if he turned into Frosty the Snowman as long as I kept cool.

Without air-conditioning, there was so much heat radiating off me that when my husband and I were in the car, the windows on my side would steam up. The bigger the baby got inside me, the more my thermostat overheated. I kept referring to my body as the Easy Bake oven, but my timer wasn't going to go off for another six weeks. The closer I got to my delivery date, the more miserable I got. Soon I just had to be naked all the time, which wasn't a pretty sight. Some people might think a naked pregnant lady is beautiful, but when I looked in the mirror I saw a sweaty, cellulite-filled, hairy-bushed, stretch-marked, miserable pregnant lady.

Let's recap: I was sweaty, unsteady, horrible to look at, and naked. It could have been worse, I suppose. I still managed to bathe so that I didn't stink. There's just got to be no sorrier sight on earth than a miserable pregnant lady who stinks!

Oh, Oh, Oh, Oh, OOOOOOOOHHHHHHH! . . . I'll Take Another One of Those, Please!

(Orgasms in Pregnancy)

Not every single thing in pregnancy was horrible, of course. There was the promise of the baby to come. And there was coming. If God has designed it that we are allowed one good thing in pregnancy, I am SO glad he picked orgasms. If you haven't had a pregnant orgasm yet, I sincerely hope that you will get to experience one in the near future. Outstanding. Capital *O*.

Now I know what you're thinking: "Who's thinking about sex? If my husband even comes near me with his penis I'm going to run." I totally understand. I was not interested in having actual sex, either, but remember, there is such a thing as "going at it alone." Know what I mean? I hope I don't have to draw you a picture.

I don't have a medical explanation for why orgasms are so much more intense when you're pregnant (something about increased blood flow, I think, but understanding it takes all the fun out of it!), and I don't really need one. I do know from checking out my expression in a mirror once that I look like I'm having a seizure during them because of the intensity. Yet another reason I avoided my husband.

Wonderful though the pregnant orgasm truly is, I would rotate from "OH YES" to "OH NO, I'M KILLING MY BABY." I constantly asked my doctor if I was harming my baby, and he constantly assured me I was not. To quiet my fears, I pictured my little baby at a Grateful Dead concert, stoned on my endorphins, just floating in ecstasy as Mom lay there with glazed eyes and a big grin.

Of course, there are some women out there who constantly crave actual sex during pregnancy. I don't know who the hell you are, but the women's magazines report that you're out there. Not me. I wanted a little Snausage maybe twice in the entire nine months of pregnancy. Other than that my husband kept his willy far away from me. Fine with me, but it was also his prerogative. He told me it felt too weird for him to have his penis banging away so close to his son. Again, fine with me. He had his dirty mags and I had the pocket rocket!

So give it a whirl and try to take advantage of the best side effect pregnancy has to offer. The big "O" is more like "O YEAH!"

The Crying Game

(Hormonal Blues)

I know I'm about to get my period every month when I'm driving alone in my car, hear a sad song on the radio, and burst into tears. It's usually some song by Barry Manilow or any Carpenters' song. Well, when you're pregnant you don't need a song to come on the radio to make you cry. You just need to hear a traffic report and the floodgates will open.

Now, I'm not talking about postpartum: That's in book two . . . heh heh heh. And I'm not talking about Psycho Chick (she's another story; see page 15). This is about all those tears shed while your bun is still in the proverbial oven. There were times I honestly thought I was going to get completely dehydrated because I would cry for days. Looking back I giggle at how emotional we women get. But those damn hormones really get the best of us. And forget about going to the movies. Even comedies made me sob.

Case in point: I was pregnant when *Moulin Rouge* came out, and I decided to treat myself to a little movie and popcorn. The big mistake here was going by myself. I cried so hard in the theater that strangers were coming up to me and asking if I was hurt. As people filed out, I hid on the ground because I couldn't control my sobbing. (Wait, it gets worse.) Once everyone had left, I ran to my car and pulled away. Seconds later I pulled over because I couldn't drive. I was sobbing so hard I began to hyperventilate. Now, if you haven't seen the movie you are probably thinking, "Damn, this must be a good flick." Well, it is a great movie, but when you're pregnant *The Wizard of Oz* would do the same thing. Hard-won advice: Take a friend with you to the movies when you're pregnant. At least you can sob on her shoulder and she can drive you home.

And here's another good piece of advice: DO NOT watch the news. Hearing about the destruction of our world does not make a woman bringing a child into it very happy. I cried without provocation. The nightly news just added fuel to the fire. Oh, and those damn baby shows. The sweet ones are good to watch (then the tears are tears of happiness), but I seemed to constantly get sucked into the ones about preemie babies needing emergency surgery. My husband would walk into the room and see my big pregnant body sobbing in front of the television and would force me to change the channel. Hard as it was to leave those little ones on the operating table, I'm grateful he yanked me out of my movie-of-the-week-induced downward spiral.

Sometimes you have no idea why you're crying. I remember sitting on the sofa watching a piece of lint roll by and I burst into tears. My husband kept asking me what was wrong, and I remember trying to think of why I was crying, but there wasn't a reason. Crying for no reason just didn't compute for him, so finally I would just make up something, as in, "I'm crying because you forgot to take the garbage out." A little cruel, sure. But a *reason* is something a man can get his head around. Offer him a reason and you get a twofer: You will get your husband off your back, and as in my case, it'll ensure that the garbage gets taken out.

So, Anyway, Like I Was Saying . . . Wait, What Was I Saying?

(Wandering Mind)

Have you experienced the "pregnancy stupids" yet? If not, believe what I say and what all the books say: It's real, it's wild, and you, too, will soon become an airhead. That's all I needed. Most people already think I've got a screw loose. And they think I've got the dumb blond thing down pat. But nothing holds a candle to the pregnancy stupids.

As I was driving in my car one glorious afternoon, I started to think about when my own mind would start to wander, when and where I would be when I'd begin to forget. It was at that point I realized I didn't need to wonder anymore. I had just passed my house by a mile and a half. How airheaded could I be? I was just driving aimlessly in thought . . . about forgetting. I couldn't believe it. A little embarrassed, a little mystified, I just giggled and figured that was as bad as things would get.

Well, by golly, I lost more brain cells every day. I couldn't remember phone numbers; I'd stand in grocery store aisles scratching my head over what I had come to buy; I'd lose my train of thought mid-conversation; once I even left my dogs at the groomer for a couple of days before I figured out they weren't simply out for a really long walk. Annoying as this clearly was, I would forget about my frustration as quickly as it popped in my head.

The flip side of losing thoughts is losing yourself in thought. Whether one of my daydreams was about playing with the baby or decorating the nursery or even about the physics of squeezing something the size of a watermelon out of my vagina, I would get sucked into my thoughts for hours. Colossal wastes of time, perhaps, but I found the daydreaming to be soothing. So remember to enjoy those daydreams and not to worry too much about being a forgetful idiot . . . that is, if you even remember this by tomorrow. In fact, you'll probably read this section over, not even remembering you read it. You airhead!

Mirror, Mirror on the Wall, Who's the Prettiest Pregnant Lady of Them All? Clearly Not You, Lady!

(Face Acne and Rashes)

Even women blessed from birth with flawless skin can have a hell of a time with breakouts when they're pregnant. My skin has always been a problem, so I knew I was in trouble. Add to my genetic predisposition the fact that I quit smoking the second I found out I was pregnant. The combination of lack of nicotine and hormonal surges made me look like someone in a bad teenage horror flick.

Not yet understandably afraid of specialists (see page 31 to refresh your memory), I went to the dermatologist desperate to get help. Even he jumped at the sight of me. Unaware of my delicate condition (pregnancy, that is), he offered me a barrage of cool-sounding drugs. But once I informed him of my condition, he laughed and said, "Suck it up, sister." NOT WHAT I WANTED TO HEAR!

Let me break it down in a little more detail for you. My entire face was filled with little zitty bumps. There wasn't one open space of good face. To top it all off, I had a red rash that circled each side of my nose down to the middle of each cheek. I was afraid that people who always saw me airbrushed for work would faint at the sight of me. Now, you might be thinking, "That's so vain." My answer to that is "Bite me." I'm human, and no one likes to be pointed to and laughed at. Because people really were pointing and laughing!

You think that movie critics are harsh, but I find that the public is worse than critics. I've actually had people walk up to me on the street and say, "God you look SO much better on TV." Even though that might be true, no one wants to hear this kind of thing! This just multiplied my fears.

The infamous "pregnancy mask" (called melasm . . . I know because I actually looked it up) is another thing to be feared among pregnant women, though I think stretch marks would win the vote for most feared skin problem (see page 77). The rash that I had was called rosacea. I'm sure you've seen the commercial about it. The medicine you take for it causes wet farts. Lovely.

Whether you get the mask or my particular rash, the key to hiding it is obvious: Wear a shitload of make-up or stop caring. Yeah, right. As if that's easy to do. Still, and as always, there's a bright side: These things definitely go away after your little chicken hatches. As a matter of fact, my skin totally rocks right now. If you see me on the street, you can make fun of my jiggly ass, but not my smooth skin.

It's a Bird! It's a Plane! . . . No, It's a Really Swollen Pregnant Lady!

(Water Retention)

As you now know, I wanted to avoid every miserable thing that happens when you're pregnant, but the swelling was one thing I particularly hoped to dodge. It just really scared me; like with getting fat, people can notice swelling, but unlike with fat, and depending on what body parts swell, you sometimes can't even hide it with clothing. Let's be honest—whether you make your living with your appearance and mediagenic-ness or not, swelling is every woman's nightmare. And looking back on it, I can see that I was worried for very good reason.

I could tell from the nurse's expression every time I went for a checkup that I was gaining more weight than I was "supposed" to. They told me I was starting to retain water. At first, you just feel like your belly looks bloated. And good for you for noticing because it is. But then, you notice that your rings are hurting your fingers. You notice that your skin is puffing up around the rings and so you decide to take them off "for a while." Well, kiss them good-bye, sister. Put them in a safe place; once they are off, you're not going to see your rings on until after you deliver or perhaps later than that. I couldn't put my rings back on until my baby was two months old. In and of itself, a little less jewelry isn't a very big deal. Except when little old men and women stare at your pregnant belly and your naked ring finger. They're putting two and two together and deciding right then and there that you're a total hussy. On more than one occasion, I wanted to show them my naked *middle* finger!

The next thing to go was my butt. Before the army of cellulite invaded, I noticed about four new inches hanging off my tail side. It was like a tray—you could place an entire TV dinner on my ass. Despite the obvious, I managed to convince myself that having "back" (as the song goes) was totally in and that I was safely in fashion. Wow! Mother Nature has a way of helping us fatties fool ourselves, doesn't she? I had a friend who, after she'd gained a good forty pounds on her belly and ass, actually said to me, "You can't really tell

I'm pregnant, can you?" No, sweetie. You've got such lovely back.

The next body part to bloat was my arms. I noticed that they were filling up the arms of sweatshirts that used to be big. Even though you can tell the difference between water and fat (water feels a lot harder to the touch than fat, and water doesn't mush around like cellulite), it wasn't a pretty sight. I said good-bye to sleeveless tops.

And then came the ankles. Or there they went. You couldn't even see my anklebones after a while. My ankles looked like giant sausage links with no definition at all.

In rapid succession, my feet were up next. I actually had rolls of skin hanging over my shoes because they swelled up so badly. Here's a little tip if you get to this stage: Your best bet is a pair of flip-flop sandals. If it's wintertime, stick to a pair of gym shoes that are one size bigger than your normal size. Either option will be comfortable and won't draw as much attention to your foot bloat.

Last but not least, and the scariest one of all is . . . pregnant head! Ah, yes. Pregnant head. Your face and head completely take on a new shape. Though this last one didn't happen to me, even your nose could expand. I once ran into an old friend who had pregnant face going, and I swear I had to really work hard to be sure it was her. Her nose was really broad and her face was a different shape. I remember thinking, "Either this is her ugly sister or she's had horrible plastic surgery."

If you are unfortunate enough to get pregnant head, I advise that you just put a paper bag over your head until you deliver or stay indoors where no one will have to see you. And I'm only half kidding! Whatever coping strategy you choose, there is cause for hope: You may feel as though you're carrying around the Pacific Ocean, but take comfort in the knowledge that the more you resemble the Michelin Tire man the closer you are to bringing your baby into the world.

The McRib Sandwich

(Back Pain)

———————————

You might be lucky enough to escape back pain. God, I hope you are. For me, back pain was more painful than delivery. And it certainly lasted longer!

My back pain really got out of hand in the sixth month. I woke up in the middle of the night with what felt like pulsing, piercing knots in the middle of my back. I kept slapping my husband to get up and rub my back, but at three o'clock in the morning he was as good as my dog. Sack of potatoes. No help at all. I know that most back pain in pregnancy is called sciatica and the pain runs down your leg (from your sciatic nerve . . . hey, I have the books too!). Mine was different but pain is pain, so hear my cry.

After a week of misery I decided that our soft-top, body-conforming mattress was the problem, and I figured that buying a new one would solve it. So off I went! I waddled into a mattress store with my credit card in one hand and a big ol' "Won't you help me, please?" smile. Of course, the combination of a ready credit card, a belly as big as a house, and an attempt to flirt basically tattoos "sucker" on your head. Live and learn. I rolled on and off a few mattresses and found one that seemed right-on. The problem was that I knew my husband, and I knew this mattress had divorce written all over it. If I got this one, he would either leave me or sleep on the couch indefinitely. But I bought it anyway. I was desperate.

When my husband came home, he saw the new mattress and decided to test it out. He took a running start and flew through the air toward it. I tried to warn him, but he was already airborne. Too late. Ka-klink! He looked like he had hit a solid piece of concrete. He reminded me of the *Roadrunner* cartoon where the coyote rams into a stone wall. He just lay there, completely still, and it looked like he was now in as much pain over the mattress as I had been when buying it. I couldn't help but giggle. And of course, things only got worse before they got better.

Once again, at 3 a.m., I woke up in horrific pain. I was howling like a dog in heat. I was crying and shaking my husband; I could hardly breathe. Bless him, he helped me get through the night with heating pads and a shitload of love (not that kind, you pervert).

The next morning we went straight to the chiropractor. I know, I know. You'd think I would have learned my lesson with seeing specialists, but this guy turned out to be a savior. He determined that my pain was due to bad posture. Once he said it, I understood immediately. To hide my pregnancy for so long I had been hunching over to hide my growing belly. Posture I could fix.

The next diagnosis was a surprise. I had popped out two ribs. TWO RIBS! Popped out?! I knew that my hips had to widen to make room for the baby; I didn't know my ribs did, too. But okay, so as my ribs were widening, some were popping out. And popping out is painful. This made sense. And ever the optimist, I kept telling myself that because I was suffering so much in my pregnancy, my delivery was going to be a cinch. (No such luck . . . read on.)

So the doc popped my ribs back in. Sounds painful but it wasn't too terribly bad. And once the ribs were back in, the back felt better. Unfortunately I had to continue to see the chiropractor every day that month because those damn ribs kept popping back out. Once, I even had to go to his house at 2 a.m. for a fix.

Of course, my husband started seeing the chiropractor because of our new mattress. The poor guy would moan all night. In a selfish way I kind of liked it. Why should I be the only one in pain all the time? Maybe husbands should have to gain all that weight, too. You know, sympathy weight.

My advice for back pain would be to get help. And I don't mean help from a mattress salesperson. Ask your doc; that's what he or she is there for. Also, pregnant massages are not only a nice treat, but they really get some of the kinks out. So treat yourself. A massage is a lot cheaper than a new mattress!

Free Gifts
for Expectant & New Moms!

We all know baby expenses can pile up. Wouldn't it be nice to get something for FREE? Let us send you FREE gifts – such as top-quality product samples, coupons and other helpful baby care information.

To receive your **FREE gifts** –
Plus a **FREE subscription** to
Babytalk magazine – simply
complete the card below
and mail it today!

babytalk

NAME _____ (PLEASE PRINT)

ADDRESS _____ APT.#

CITY _____ STATE ___ ZIP

EMAIL (OPTIONAL) _____

▶ Your child's expected or actual date of birth: Month ___ Year ___
▶ Is this your first child? ☐ Yes ☐ No
▶ Would you like a **FREE subscription** to Babytalk magazine? ☐ Yes ☐ No

If yes, simply sign and date.

YAA0J6

Act now for your
free gifts!

BUSINESS REPLY MAIL
FIRST-CLASS MAIL   PERMIT NO. 22   TAMPA FL

POSTAGE WILL BE PAID BY ADDRESSEE

babytalk

PO BOX 62623
TAMPA FL 33662-6231

Headaches
(Headaches . . . Duh)

─────────────────

Not all headaches are created equal. I've had headaches before, but no one prepared me for what pregnancy could deliver. It was as though a jackhammering troll had moved into my head.

It all began around the tenth week of pregnancy. I was sitting on the couch watching television and kaboom! I clutched my head and screamed. My husband thought I was having a brain aneurysm. I thought I had about two minutes left to live. If I hadn't been pregnant, I would have sliced my head off. Now, I know what you're thinking: "Get a grip on yourself . . . we get it." But the pain, I tell you, was HORRIFIC! The only relief was a Tylenol and a heating pad for my neck. That took a whole 2 percent of the pain away. I was then left trying to figure out what to do with the other 98 percent. This went on for about two months. On someone's advice, I started doubling up on my prenatal vitamins, and that helped until I got completely constipated again. These headaches are supposedly "normal" in pregnancy, so don't freak out like I did and think you're dying. Once again, our hormones are raging, causing the brain to throb. Just hang in there, partner; the best is yet to come!

That Ain't My Ass!

(Cellulite Gain)

Before I became pregnant, I told myself that I was going to eat healthy and work out religiously, and that I would be a cute pregnant lady. I wanted to look like Madonna when she was pregnant. Wishful thinking. I did manage to work out: At its height, my workout regimen consisted of one hour of cardio every day and two days a week of weights. I hate to break it to you, but even all this did NOTHING to keep cellulite off my ass!

Let's be honest. Most women already have some amount of cellulite. From years of yo-yoing weight, I have my fair share, too (airbrushing is a great invention!). But pregnant cellulite takes things to a whole new level. It's ridiculous.

I think I first noticed my problem on my normal morning waddle to the toilet. On the way there I passed my bedroom mirror. Just like in the movies, I did a double take, and I waddled my ass backward to find myself in the mirror again. I could not believe my eyes. That wasn't my ass! It was seriously three times the size of its usual bulbous state, and it was loaded with cottage cheese. And I mean LOADED! What the hell? I didn't waddle to the gym every day for this.

My husband also noticed a different shape to it that day. He kept humming the song "Baby's Got Back." I soon became obsessed. When I would walk down the street, I would stare at the reflection of my ass in store windows. Then I would look down and see that my shadow's ass even looked skinnier than mine. I was demoralized, and my workouts slowly became nonexistent. I could hardly breathe anyway with my lungs being squashed by my growing baby. I knew I had to try to surrender and accept my new ass.

Well, I tried. I tried really hard. But it didn't work altogether. In the end, I just avoided turning around in the mirror to view my back end altogether. This did make things a little easier. I knew it was there, but at least I didn't have to witness new cottage cheese dimples forming every day. Out of sight, sort of out of mind.

When I did get too hard on myself (which was quite often), I would stare at my pregnant belly and kind of hug and rock it. Reminding myself that there was a good reason for all this change and heartache made those tough moments just a little easier to deal with. Not easy. But easier.

No, Not Yet!
I'm Not Ready for This Yet!
(Premature Labor)

You might be thinking that premature labor is rare or at least that it's not going to happen to you. Let me tell you: It's not and it might, sister. Don't skip this part. And don't ignore the warning signs.

In my twenty-fifth week of pregnancy I decided to treat myself to a day of beauty. You know, a pamper thyself day. First up, I went to get a pretty blow-dry from my hair stylist. While I was there, I started feeling crampy, but I just blew it off, thinking it was my ol' uterus growing. As he continued to "blow me out" (sounds nice, eh?), I started sweating. He saw my glow and asked me if I was okay. I really wasn't sure myself, so I called my husband, who assured me (doctor that he isn't) that my uterus was probably just growing (great minds think alike). So I tried to ignore my cramps, tipped my hairdresser, and drove to the manicurist. While I was getting my nails buffed, I started feeling worse. My cramps were getting stronger and seemed to be starting a pattern (like every five minutes). Something told me that these weren't those Braxton Hicks contractions everyone told me about (you know, the ones that certainly feel weird but don't really hurt). I asked my Vietnamese manicurist, who'd just had a baby, what labor pains feel like. She didn't speak much English, so all she kept saying was "Legs hurt real bad, legs hurt real bad." Needless to say that didn't help much, so I had her stop, and I got the hell out of there. Halfway home I realized that I could barely drive. Safe barely-driving driver that I am, I took one hand off the wheel and called my husband. I told him to meet me at home because I was sure that something was seriously wrong.

I know what you're thinking: "She thought something was seriously wrong, so why didn't she just drive to the hospital?" The reason is that these cramps felt exactly like menstrual cramps. In fact I'd had worse period cramps than this, so I convinced myself that I was doing fine. Women in labor scream and yell, and I wasn't doing that. But when I finally got home, I started puffing like you see laboring women do in movies, and I started to panic. I called my doctor, who told me to have a glass of wine and put my feet up. What the #%*# kind of loony advice is that? To this day, I don't know the medical explanation!

As soon as I hung up the phone, I looked at my husband and told him to get me to the hospital. Pulling up to the emergency room when you are only twenty-five weeks pregnant is like pulling up with a gunshot wound. It's made-for-TV drama. People rush all around you and zoom you away for help. They'll do anything to prevent a premature birth, which I'm so grateful for.

Once I was inside, they hooked a belt across my belly to hear the baby's heartbeat and to monitor my contractions. What those things told them is that I was indeed in labor. My heart sank as visions of sick pre-emie babies poured through my mind from watching all those scary medical shows, the ones that had made me cry like a baby myself. My memory is a little foggy about all this, but I'm pretty sure I told anyone who would listen that they were welcome to sew up my vagina to keep the baby inside (okay, so it's the cervix that counts, but *vagina* is the word I used).

Sewing me up turned out not to be necessary. I wasn't dilating and my water hadn't broken, so the chances were good that they could stop my labor. They gave me an injection of something, and it made me feel like I was having a seizure. My head was bouncing all around uncontrollably and my hands were quivering. I could tell by my husband's face that he was totally freaked out. But I wasn't that worried. I figured I was in good hands and this seizure-inducing stuff was helping my baby. After about four hours, when the contractions finally ended, they released me.

I went home and took it easy for the remaining fifteen weeks. I kind of put myself on bed rest. Better to be safe than sorry. I wasn't going to let anything happen to my little chicken.

Moral of the story: Listen to your body, not a manicurist, and maybe not even your doc. If I had listened to him, I would have been a drunken pregnant lady giving birth at home on my brand-new, expensive, rock-hard mattress.

Poopin' on the Table

(The Dark Side of Delivery)

———————————

NO ONE EVER TALKS ABOUT THIS! Or should I say no one ever told me about this. I want to talk about it. I want you to know about it: You might just take a crap on the delivery room table. Yes, right there in front of the crowd of doctors and nurses who have gathered for the blessed event. The blessed crap. Clearly, there is no justice in this world.

I freaked out when my mother once said in passing, "I hope you don't poopie on the table, dear." I was astonished. I was like "What the hell are you talking about, Ma?" She went on to tell me that when you are pushing during delivery, you "bear down" just like you do when you're going Number Two and that sometimes you push out a little poopie. I handled back pain and rib popping and nasty red face rashes and more, but this I couldn't handle.

I proceeded to ask every woman who had ever given birth if she had pooped on the table, and I was horrified to learn that almost every woman I asked had actually had it happen. I was freaking out at the thought of this. My friends couldn't believe how worried I was about this, considering that under different circumstances, poop is one of my favorite topics. Under different circumstances is the operative phrase there, folks!

I continued to bug my mother about this, and she kept assuring me that it's no big deal because they whisk it away so quickly (now there's a job for ya . . . Do the nurses know this will be one of their tasks when they sign on to work in labor and delivery?). And by that point in delivery, she said, you could really care less. She had given birth to four girls, she had pooped on the table almost every time . . . and she had never mentioned this. Ah, but now that she'd opened the floodgates, she shared another beautiful detail with me: Hers were like logs. I was like "MA, NO WAY! Stop scaring me."

So, as with all my concerns, off I went to my gynecologist and shared my big fear with him. He kind of smiled and told me he could understand my worry.

This told me that yes, indeed, it could happen. He'd seen it before. He suggested that if my water hadn't broken by the time I was ready to go to the hospital, I could give myself an enema. He also told me that when women go into labor, the body anticipates the problem and sometimes cleans itself out naturally. You know, kind of like a self-cleaning oven (my comparison, not his). Indeed, he continued, it can be a warning that labor will start soon if your bowels become more active.

Well, I was hoping my bowels would be on full alert and very cooperative, but just in case, I had an enema under the sink ready to go. Keep reading to find out if I needed it or if I pooped on the table. Believe me, one way or another, there's more shit to come.

The Blue Twinkies

(Your Swollen Vagina)

———————————————

Blue Twinkies does not refer to your vagina after delivery. That would be called Blown-Out Vagina. This section is about the evolution of your vagina in *preparation* for blowing it out. Though I really do find the vagina fascinating, I promise I'm not going to get all *Vagina Monologues* on you here. Those girls talk about the vagina like it's got feelings and needs a wardrobe!

For years I've been getting my bikini area totally waxed. That includes any hair that might be lurking in the darkest regions. All things being equal, I have to say I've taken pretty good care of myself *down there.* Then one day I couldn't see anything in that region anymore due to my growing belly. So I decided to take a break from waxing, a well-deserved break. I figured since I really wasn't having sex with my husband, why worry about how pretty my hoo-hoo looks? So days turned into weeks, and weeks turned into months, and my crotch turned into the South American Jungle. It still didn't bother me. After all, I couldn't see it.

What DID bother me was when I went to wipe one day and noticed that things felt a bit puffy down there. Feeling curious I decided to take a peek. Considering I couldn't see a damn thing without help, I pulled a mirror out from under the bathroom sink and took a looksee. Holy shit! If I had been standing, I would have staggered. What the hell was going on? My labia (those flappy things) looked like two blue Twinkies cuddling under really bad carpeting.

How could no one have warned me about this? I've come to find out that I wasn't abnormal. Your hoo-hoo becomes engorged with blood when you're pregnant, and that can sometimes cause swelling and a bluish or purplish coloration. Not everyone is lucky enough to go through this. But check yours out for yourself, and if you dare, ask around. I'll bet a stack of cash that lots of women have looked and that "Blue Twinkies" best describes the sight. Whether anyone is willing to talk about it is another matter entirely.

Die, Model Bitch, Die!

(Hating Skinny People)

During your pregnancy you will begin to despise skinny people, especially hot skinny people or, more accurately, hot skinny celebrities showing off their hot bods on TV. Yes, even I was incredibly jealous of them as I sat—weighing in at a good 182—watching TV with my husband. When they would come on the screen, I would sneak a peek at him to monitor his reaction. Just as I thought: Drool leaked out from the corner of his mouth. Someone needs to tell those damn Victoria's Secret models to try a little something called food. Meow! I'll say it again, if men only knew how hard this was on us, they would bow to us for the entire nine months.

Here's an incident (well, at least I made it an "incident") of note. My husband and I were watching some quality TV: a show that had Playmates competing for some type of cash prize. Having absolutely no stomach for those tight, smooth bodies, I tried to switch the channel. Of course, I was stopped the moment my hand touched the remote. My husband was determined to watch. So I did what any red-blooded American girl would do: I made serious fun of all the girls. My husband behaved liked every red-blooded American man and stared at them like they were the first women he'd ever seen in his life.

Right before a commercial break, they previewed what was coming up next: While getting wet, the playmates removed their clothes, revealing skimpy swimsuits. I went mad. I told my husband I couldn't take it. He said I was being silly, considering I had been a Playmate once myself. Well, if I had known what the sight of a Playmate did to women during pregnancy, I would have done us all a favor and been the fattest and hairiest Playmate of all time.

The show came back on, and there they were, all stripping down into skimpy bikinis. I begged my husband to switch the damn channel! He refused. I begged some more. I told him I couldn't sit there and watch beautiful skinny women while I looked down at my knee-sized ankles. He clearly couldn't understand what the hell I was going through, and I didn't have the energy for Psycho Chick, so I resorted to the only thing I knew that would work. I began crying. It worked. We switched to the Disney channel.

Another effective strategy and one that feels devilishly good is this: While your husband is getting undressed at night, look in a magazine and shout out, "Damn! That George Clooney has a fine ass!" See how he likes it.

OOOOH! I Think I Felt the Baby Move . . . or Maybe It's Just Gas

(Baby Kicks)

────────────────

This was a moment I couldn't wait for. After going through the hardships of my first trimester, I couldn't wait to be rewarded with a little kick. Of course, at first it's more like a butterfly fluttering, and if you're not paying attention, you might think it's just gas. The difference: Gas is nasty, kicking is wonderful.

I felt the first movement at about sixteen weeks. I was sitting on the sofa watching TV (again!) when I felt this little flutter. I knew it was the baby and I lit up with happiness. Yeah, we all see the ultrasounds, but nothing can prepare you for the first flutter in your belly. At this point you feel even more connected to your baby, and it makes you want to start eating more vegetables. Your precious cargo just became more precious.

It was hard for my husband to relate to this because it was too soon for him to feel anything from the outside. But once he got his turn, it was fun to watch him freak out. When the baby got bigger and the kicks were much more intense, I would put his hand on my belly and watch his face light up. I'm sure it was rewarding for him after the drama I'd put him through those first few months.

Looking back, some of my fondest memories were the times I would sit alone on my couch (ah, the couch again) and feel my baby moving about. I would place my hand on my belly and sing him little songs. It was our time together and I loved every minute of it. That said, it drove me crazy when he got hiccups. I hate getting them myself, but when you feel them—your belly jerks a little every time—but aren't the one having them, it's too strange.

It wasn't until a friend of mine taught me how to put a positive spin on baby hiccups that I started to actually enjoy them. She explained that one way of thinking about it was that hiccups were a way for the baby to tell us that he was okay in his little home. The hiccups were his sign for "Everything's okay, Ma!"

Needless to say, from this point on I LOVED his little hiccups.

Enjoy it while you can because the hiccups and kicks are going to turn into less endearing little cries before you know it!

Organizing Freak

(Your Nesting Instinct)

As with animals in the wild, the pregnant human female will one day have the uncontrollable urge to get her little nest in order. I kept reading about this and wondering when my time would come, when my instinct would kick in. I was in my eighth month and still calmly looking past jammed and unorganized closets. Then came the ninth month of pregnancy, and all I have to say is move over, Alice from the *The Brady Bunch,* cuz my organizing bitch took over. I would get these bursts of energy and pace the house like a caged animal looking for things to clean and organize. After I organized the jammed closets and drawers in a twenty-four-hour period, I searched the house for more to do.

Then I realized I needed to get my baby's family tree in order. An essential thing to do, right? I got pictures of my husband's family, combined them with mine, included both our baby pictures, and made album after album of our genetic history. It'd probably be years until our son cared about these, but I had to do it. There was just no stopping me.

After that task was completed, I thought it would be a great idea to move furniture around. Picture my big pregnant body, wearing my muumuu, sliding a seven-foot bookshelf across the room. My husband screamed as he saw me in his peripheral vision. But that didn't seem to stop me. I rearranged the nursery at least seven times, and when my husband made me promise I wouldn't touch another thing in the house, I moved to the front yard and started moving giant potted plants. There was no end to this until I left for the hospital to deliver a few weeks later.

In retrospect, of course, I highly recommend *not* moving giant pieces of furniture around. But take advantage of the less dangerous forms of your nesting instinct . . . you won't be seeing an organized junk drawer again any time soon.

Breathing for Dummies
(Lamaze)

———————————

Lamaze . . . you can take it or leave it. I have to tell you: I left it. Literally. And I'm guilt-free about my decision, so all you women out there who swear by it (and I have found that those of you who do really do!) might well want to skip this part.

In my defense, I tried to like it, I tried to get the hang of it, but Lamaze just didn't do it for me. Of course, I was sucked into giving it a whirl because everyone told me I would be lost without the famous Lamaze breathing and relaxation techniques during labor. Who wants to be lost? I signed up.

I should have known from the start that this was not for me. My first nightmare was simply getting into a class. They all were booked and pricey. I heard about private, in-the-privacy-of-your-own-home Lamaze classes, but I was afraid that a one-on-one would force me to pay real attention. See, my heart just wasn't in this!

Finally, I found a class with an opening that was held in a church basement. So off we went, my husband and me, to our first Lamaze class. The first thing I did—and you will, too, don't kid yourself—was scope out the other pregnant women and count how many of them had bigger asses than me. Then I relayed the tally to my husband so he could feel proud sitting next to my big-but-not-the-biggest ass.

Next, our instructor—a woman who, with her earth mother skirt and low-hanging, bra-less boobs could have been pulled from a *Saturday Night Live* sketch of childbirth class—announced that we would first see a video of a birth to get our feet wet.

Before I go on, I simply must say this: Can someone please tell me why all of these birthing tapes show a woman giving birth with a circa 1970 overgrown bush? Come on! Can't they update these things with some well-trimmed real estate? (Okay, okay; as you saw a little earlier, I eventually gained some empathy for the free-range look.)

Anyway, the birthing tape wasn't that shocking or educational. My husband and I agreed that we had learned more watching pregnancy shows on TV. Some of the other couples looked a little queasy, but they may have just been bored and hungry.

Following the tape we began to learn about contractions—what they are, when you know they're real. If memory serves, my husband and I fell asleep on each other at this point. We woke up at break time. And we looked at each other and knew it was time to escape. We snuck out the back door and were a little giddy. We felt just like two kids ditching school.

Now that I've gone through labor, I know that with an epidural, Lamaze breathing techniques are basically useless. That is, if they get the epidural administered right, you won't be in pain. Certainly not enough pain to have to go sheesh, sheesh, shooooo at every contraction.

Still, I can appreciate the fear of the unknown, and a childbirth prep class might help calm your nerves. But for goodness sake, try to find a prep class that teaches you something about taking care of your newborn instead of endless advice about taking care of your vagina. If this book has taught you anything so far, I hope it's that in the vagina department, you have to let nature take its course.

What the Fu*k Are These?
(Stretch Marks)

Though there are lots of things to worry about during pregnancy, I think that stretch marks are, for many women, the most dreaded. I mean, they're permanent! They fade to your skin color, but they are still there. How terrifying is that?

To women who escape getting stretch marks, I offer you lukewarm congratulations. No, scratch that. I actually hate you.

Stretch marks look like a cat crawled up on your body and stuck its claws into your skin and slowly scraped down an inch or more leaving a reddish or purplish squiggly indented line. They can develop any-where on your body just because you gain weight (pregnant or not), but most pregnant women watch them appear on their growing bellies.

I think I first saw them when I was watching those pregnancy shows on TV called *Maternity Ward* and *Baby Story*. These pregnant women would lift up their blouses for their ultrasound, and I would shriek! They'd have these horrible marks.

Terrified, I doused my body in oil every day. An old wives' tale, I know, but I gave it a try all the same. My theory on the virtue of oiling yourself goes like this: If your mom had stretch marks in her pregnancy, then you have a good chance of getting them yourself, with or without oil. If she didn't, your chances of avoiding them look pretty good. In other words, oil may only serve to make you *feel* more in control of the process.

Proof of its value or not, there are many women who swear by their oil. If you want to join them in lathering up, go ahead. At the very least, it's good for moisturizing your skin. And it feels good. In fact, I would make my husband oil me up at night until I got so fat that I started to feel like a side of bacon preparing to be fried up. That vision took the fun out of it for me. And read on for more about pigs in the bedroom.

Now, perhaps you're wondering if I ended up getting the dreaded marks. Yes, I did. I got them on my boobs and my ass, but not my belly. So I got half lucky.

But I don't look at my ass anymore. And I'm sure I won't again until they come out with a magic cream or a new treatment. Plastic surgeons say they can reduce stretch marks now with a laser. Well, buddy, I want them GONE, not reduced, so work a little harder on a cure, will ya?

I Just Need to Lie Down for, Like, Five Minutes . . . Okay, Maybe Three Months

(Sleepiness)

Imagine staying up all night, then running a marathon, then doing three hundred loads of laundry and raking leaves off a football field all in one day. How tired would you be? That's how tired I felt EVERY DAY in my first trimester. It's like someone snuck in and stole all the juice out of my body. Our bodies give so much to the embryo I'm surprised we can even get off the couch. As you've read, I didn't get off mine much. Literally, I could barely talk. My friends would call me in the afternoon and I would sound drunk because I was so tired. My goal every day was to at least try to make it through an entire hour of Oprah without falling asleep.

I worked throughout my pregnancy, but my line of work isn't all day every day. I couldn't imagine working a nine-to-five shift. To all those women out there who do, I worship you. And I hope someone offers you a rest on a couch or a nap every day. If you have to stand at your job, make sure you demand a chair. And this goes for early on when you aren't showing, too. You might not look pregnant this early in the game, but your body will remind you every second you stand there.

As my husband is fond of reminding me, I got so tired while pregnant that I sometimes started snoring in mid-conversation. I would be sitting up in bed, talking to him, and then, clunk . . . I was out. There were also times when I could feel it coming on. It felt like a giant wave would be headed my way. Out of the blue I would say, "Uh oh." My husband knew exactly what that meant and would walk me to bed. Those were the best naps in the whole world. Ever full of great advice, my mom told me to enjoy those naps because if and when I get pregnant with Baby Number Two, those naps will be nonexistent; there's no rest for the weary when there's a toddler to chase around the house.

The amazing thing about my sleepiness is that it completely disappeared at the end of my first trimester.

I remember reading that I would wake up one day refreshed, with a surge of energy. And it actually happened. I don't know why I was all that surprised—the books had been right about a lot of things. But even with warning, it's an amazing feeling. This is a good time to get all your stuff done before you turn into the Goodyear blimp, like registering and decorating your nursery, because when that last trimester begins, guess what comes back? You got it . . . the sandman, and he brings a shitload of sand!

Pig in the Pasture

(Sex in the Ninth Month)

I don't think pigs graze in pastures, but I just figured it sounded better than "pig in the mud." Any way you phrase it, this is exactly how I felt the one and only time my husband and I had sex in the ninth month. All the books tell you about "comfortable positions," and the one they really zero in on is the "doggy-style" position. Sure, it's great at an ideal weight, but when you're close to two hundred pounds, you aren't thinking dog . . . you're thinking pig. And I'm sure I sounded like one because my cries (of joy and desire, of course) sounded more like squeals than oohs and ahs. It was clear to me that my poor husband was concentrating hard on his Rolodex of fantasies because I sure as hell wasn't one for him anymore. I just wanted that piggy sex to end, but I hung in there like a good wife because I wanted to take care of my man. (Full disclosure: I was really "bad" the whole pregnancy. I never really "took care of him." I should have offered a couple of blow jobs here and there, but the way I felt every day, you couldn't have paid me enough.)

Now, let me give you a better visual. My husband is very lean. Sexy as hell. But very lean. Most women would kill for his metabolism. As I propped myself into position and we began to get down, I could feel that his entire lean body was half the size of my ass. No joke. I couldn't stop thinking that his skinny frame was going to get stuck between my ass cheeks. So every time I felt him pump, I would clench my cheeks to keep from swallowing him up. All the while, I couldn't stop thinking how just plain wrong this was. This was not a high-self-esteem moment for a pregnant woman in desperate need of some. My advice: If you're not feeling it, don't try this one. Leave it to some lonely farmer.

The Moment of Truth

(Labor and Delivery)

After reading all that's come before, you might think I could have caught a break in the labor and delivery arena. I mean, I'd endured enough hardships, don't you think? No freaking way. In fact, just writing this section makes me cry as I relive the end of the journey. Don't worry; I'll still make you laugh, but I have to warn you that in this section I actually take you to a serious place for once. Here I go . . . My name is Jenny and this is my story.

I woke up one Friday morning in May feeling my usual miserable self. But I noticed that on this particular day I was a tad more miserable than usual. I rolled off my firm mattress and noticed that I was having multiple Braxton Hicks contractions. I knew it was them because they didn't hurt, but I was getting them every few minutes. Then I waddled to the bathroom and noticed my bowels were really awake and eager to be used. As I sat on the toilet, it occurred to me that I might be starting labor. It was just about my due date, after all.

So what does one do? Well, any normal person would tell her husband to be on full alert, and she would make sure her bags were packed and yadda yadda. Not me. No, I called and made a hair appointment because I wanted a nice blow-dry for all of my delivery pictures. Yes, I'm an idiot.

Off I went to the hair salon, and as cosmic punishment I immediately started to feel crampy. I sat through my blow-dry even though my hairstylist told me I was crazy and needed to get home (remember, this was the guy who had witnessed my false labor months before). I suffered through the final stages of grooming sweating and moaning. When I finally made it home, I couldn't lie down because I was too eager, and I knew we still had some time before we should go to the hospital. No longer Psycho Chick and with a surprising presence of mind, I remembered the "4-1-1 rule" that my doctor had drilled into my head: My contractions needed to be four minutes apart, one minute long, for one hour before I went to the hospital.

I needed to kill time. I snuck into the bathroom and pulled out my waiting enema. It looked mean and foreign and invasive, but I thought hard about using it. Remember, my big fear was not if I was going to tear my vagina on the table but if I POOPED ON THE TABLE. After standing in the bathroom for ten minutes having contractions and feeling miserable, I came to the conclusion that the last thing I wanted to do was to stick something up my butt. So, I threw the enema away. Little did I know I was also throwing away any hope of having a poop-free delivery.

Finally, at midnight, my contractions were 4-1-1, so we ventured off to the hospital with our suitcase and our nervous bellies. On the drive there my husband and I talked about how we felt like we were standing on the edge of the Grand Canyon and didn't know whether to fly or fall in. We were absolutely terrified about what was to come. We understood that this would be the last time that life was only about the two of us. In a few hours we would be responsible for another life. No more clowning around. As Dr. Phil would say, "It's time to get real, people." We looked at each other and smiled, and when we arrived at the hospital, we were whisked off to labor and delivery.

From there, things slowed down. As when I was in premature labor, they hooked me up with belts to monitor the baby's heart and measure contractions. My sweet little nurse asked if I wanted to get hooked up with an epidural yet. This part was confusing for me because I wasn't in severe amounts of pain, but I'd heard those horror stories about women who waited too long and couldn't get an epidural. Then there were the stories about the women who got it too early and it ran out right before they were about to push. I asked her if she thought I was close to pushing, and she laughed and said, "Darlin', it's midnight, and you probably won't start pushing until three in the afternoon." So I figured I would wait on the epidural. I wasn't too anxious for a needle in my back anyway.

After about an hour, now feeling settled in our room, I started to envision myself giving birth and . . . completely started to freak out. I almost hyperventilated. I realized that this wasn't one of the million daydreams I'd had during pregnancy. This was real. I became terrified at the thought of pushing a giant head through my vagina, and I was certain that my vagina would be the only one in the world not up to the challenge. How could it be? My vagina would never be able to open to a gaping hole the size of a watermelon. My husband was trying to calm me down, but it wasn't working. I was just too scared.

I decided that my peace of mind lay with an epidural. I devised a plan, before the anesthesiologist walked in, to flirt with him so he would give me extra medicine. This goes to show you that I did indeed fall asleep during my one Lamaze class. Had I been listening, I would have known that a machine on a timer, not a person, dispenses the epidural medicine throughout your labor.

After what seemed like an eternity, a tired-looking resident walked in with his epidural gear, and I started working my charm. For some reason, I thought I was still this 125-pound girl wearing fake eyelashes. NO, I was a 185-pound massive whale with pasty, pale skin trying to "work it" with my anesthesiologist. Needless to say, the little man was not "getting it" but did do a great job administering the epidural. Surprisingly, it didn't hurt like I thought it would. It stung for about ten seconds and went away. And then the fun began. All the cramping below my waist disappeared. What a miracle! My husband tells me that it was at that point that I smiled for the first time since checking into the hospital.

The nurse told me to try to rest because it was 2 a.m., and I needed to save my strength. Strength? Then reality hit again. Things had only really just begun. I still had to squeeze a giant head through my vagina. Once again I started to panic. My husband was folded up in the shape of a pretzel on a tiny chair, snoring. I stared quietly at the ceiling trying to figure out a way to get out of this. I honestly didn't believe I could go through with the delivery, and I reminded myself that it was still early. The nurse said I probably wouldn't push until the afternoon, so I figured I would try to postpone my panic until then.

Every fifteen minutes a nurse would come check on me, so even if I thought I could get some shut-eye, it would've been impossible. The big hand on the clock moved to an erect position, making it exactly 4 a.m., and I started to feel something weird going on down there. I thought I'd peed on myself, but I had a catheter (a convenience I loved, by the way, and you will, too), so I knew that couldn't be it. My eyes bugged out when I realized what this was. My water had broken! I shouted for my husband and kept yelling, "My water broke, honey; my water broke, honey!" All I got back was a grizzly bear snore. He was out for the count. Give me some of whatever he took!

I rang the nurse and she confirmed what I was thinking. (By the way, be extremely nice to your nurses, and they will reciprocate. Mine were clearly getting bitched at by the woman in the next room, and I could tell that they were giving it right back to her. Be friendly and give them respect . . . your hospital experience will be so much better!)

With the broken water now confirmed, the nurse proceeded to tell me that, because my water had broken, my contractions would get stronger and that active labor was now upon me. So what did I do? I started freaking out again. The clock seemed to be ticking awfully loud. Most women want to hurry up and get labor over with, but not me. I wanted the guy from *The Twilight Zone* to come out and stop time completely. My mom was flying out to be with us and wouldn't get to the hospital until noon. I needed her badly. I was counting on her to help me or at least help me run away.

Fast-forward a bit (though again, it was an eternity) to 9 a.m. I hadn't had one minute of sleep. My nails were mere nubs; I had been biting them all night and especially vigorously when they checked my dilation. The epidural was working, so pain wasn't an issue. (How can you not get one of those?) At this point I was dilated to four, and my husband was STILL asleep. Denial is a powerful sleep aid, I guess!

In the next hour my family started to show up. First, my mother-in-law, whom I adore, followed by my sisters and then the most beautiful radiant human being that ever walked the face of the earth: my mother. She fell into my arms, and I gripped her hard, like we were about to go upside down on a roller coaster. I told her how terrified I was, and she calmed me by stroking my hair as only a mother can do.

Then it was noon, and once again, I felt something weird going on down there. For lack of a better way to describe it, I tell you that I felt this enormous grapefruit sliding down my vagina walls. No pain, just pressure. Lots of pressure. I looked at my mother with big watery eyes and asked her what the hell was going on. She smiled and said the baby was moving down into position and that I was probably close to being able to push. But I was sure I was not ready to push. It seemed like just minutes before I had been only four centimeters dilated.

I rang the nurse and asked her to check me again. Sure enough, Mom was right: I was dilated eight of the needed ten centimeters, so they called my doctor to tell him to be on his way. My husband finally woke from the dead and tried to comfort me. In fact, my whole family was now around me, but that didn't stop the terror of what was to come shortly. MORE PRESSURE was building, and I heard this beeping going off next to me. I asked the nurse what it was, and she calmly smiled and said, "Oh, that's your epidural machine; it ran out."

My reply: "WHAT!? YOU'VE GOT TO BE KIDDING ME. NO FREAKING WAY. YOU DON'T UNDERSTAND. I CAN'T DEAL WITH FEELING ANYTHING, NOT EVEN A LITTLE ACHE. GET SOMEBODY IN HERE NOW!"

She told me I was too close to pushing and that I needed to feel a little pain in order to push. But I told her in order to get me to push, she had better get that epidural going again. My doctor now joined the party, and I begged him to give me more if I promised to push better than any woman he had ever seen. He smiled and agreed, though I'm not really sure that he did give me more!

When—shortly thereafter—I was dilated to ten centimeters, the doctor told me it was game time. The family surrounded me, with my mom holding one leg and my mother-in-law holding the other. What a sight we must have been.

I started to push and realized I had no idea if I actually was pushing, because I was so numb down there. I didn't say anything for fear they would take the epidural away. So I just pushed really hard like I was trying to go to the bathroom ... bathroom??? Immediately I thought, "Holy shit! Am I pooing on the table? I have no idea because I can't feel anything down there." Fortunately, that particular panic lasted only two seconds. At that point it was as my mother had said it would be: I could have filled the room with poo and could have cared less. (I came to find out that I did fill the room with it ... my husband broke the news to me at a much later date.)

My doc and nurses told me I was a great pusher (there's nothing like "pleasing the teacher" to make you want to try harder!). They also told me to save some energy and to try to rest between contractions. I think it was at about this time that I noticed my body temperature rising. I yelled at my husband to get a wet cloth.

He came back with a corner of the cloth wet. Well, I lost it and yelled at him to "soak the fucking thing in ice because I'm fucking dying."

More pushing, and the doc said he could see the head through the canal. Though it kind of surprised me, all of my sisters decided to cruise down there and take a peek. I watched their faces to see how excited they would be. Instead, they looked like they'd just seen a grotesque horror show and covered their faces and ran away. Understandable but certainly NOT THE REACTION I HAD HOPED FOR.

Now I was exhausted through and through. I had been up all night and hadn't even had any energy when we'd started. As the hours went by, I was passing out between contractions. My husband was throwing ice on my body and my head (so much for that blow-dry) because I was becoming delirious. At one point, I managed to open one eye and saw the look on my mom's face and knew something was wrong. I looked down between my legs and saw that they were using a vacuum to try and get my baby out. All of my fears were coming true. I knew my vagina was not meant to get a head through it! As the doctor pulled the vacuum cord with all of his might, a nurse laid her entire body on my stomach trying to push the baby out. This was like battlefield labor and delivery!

My mom was crying, I was screaming, and my sisters looked purple. I was completely out of ammo and could no longer physically push. My doctor told me I had been pushing for two-and-a-half hours and it was time to start talking about a C-section. I raised my head with all of my might and said, "What the hell are we waiting for?"

What happened next is kind of a blur. I was prepped and wheeled to an operating room. On the way there, I was partly unconscious. Not from any drugs, just pure exhaustion. I could hear the people talking around me as they started to wheel me down the hall faster. I heard a nurse say that the baby's heart rate was dropping. I was so out of it, I couldn't even mutter an "oh no." They literally threw me on the table, slapped some disinfectant on, and began. My husband was at my side, and I could see the terror in his face as we heard the nurse shouting out that the baby's heart rate had dropped in half. Thirty seconds later they pulled the baby out and unwound the cord that was wrapped around his neck. I lay there strapped to the table, paralyzed from the neck down. Crucified.

They whisked the baby off to the side of the room in a panic. I've come to find out that with C-sections, they usually show you your baby over the curtain and tell you the sex. They didn't do that for me, and I guessed that something was wrong. Tears were streaming down my face. I looked at my husband and asked him what was wrong. He looked just as panicked as I did and said, "I don't know, honey."

A nurse moved out of the way, and I saw my baby lying on a table, blue and not moving. People were all around, giving him oxygen, slapping him, saying, "Come on, little man, breathe." That's when I stopped breathing. It's cliché because it's so true: The world went into slow motion as a minute went by with no baby cries. My husband was pale as a sheet. If it weren't really happening to me, I'd have thought this was a bad TV movie.

All of a sudden I heard a "waa waa." He was crying! I wanted to jump up and down and scream, but I was still tied to the table. My husband walked over to the baby and ran back to me to tell me how cute he was. Then he went back to the baby to introduce himself. On my side of the room, nerves, medication, and exhaustion set in, and I began vomiting all over the place. Another lovely sight. But I didn't care what the hell happened to me as long as my baby was okay.

Once they had our baby all cleaned up and ready for his closeup, my husband walked over to me and showed me my little boy wrapped like a burrito. I cried and cried. They unstrapped my hand so I could touch his little cheek and give him a peck. I couldn't believe my eyes. I said, "Look at him, honey; he blinks." To see the baby blink and look at you makes it so much more real than kicks in your belly. Chills came over my body as I started to feel a new chamber in my heart growing. My husband's face glowed like he had seen the gates of heaven open, and we stared in awe at the most beautiful thing we had ever seen.

Life was good. Life was going to be great. I had plans for this boy. I would fill him with so much love that he'd be able to conquer the world. Watching my husband glow with love also took my breath away. I don't think he had enough room in his body to contain the amount of love he was feeling at that point. Our baby was alive and well, and we adored him.

Having a child is life-changing and so incredibly beautiful. You are about to experience the best of what life has to offer . . . the ability to GIVE life . . . and frankly, I'm jealous of the intensity and joy you will be feeling. I had a rough year, but as I said at the start, I would do it all over again in a second, and maybe I will . . .

Welcome to the best job you will ever have: mommyhood.

Let Me Repeat

(Husband No-No's)

On the following page is a list of advice for your husband. Actually, it's a short list of things he'd be well-advised to take to heart. Scratch that. These are his marching orders! Ever thoughtful of your needs, I put these specifics on the following pages so you can rip them out and stick them on the refrigerator. Notice that this advice is also written to him as though it were from you. My feeling here is that none of us can afford to be *too* clear on these issues. This way your beloved will know exactly what you need from him during these growing months. Who knows, maybe these directions will help him help you keep Psycho Chick at bay.

Take My Advice . . .

- Do not stare or gawk at another woman or compliment the way she looks. I know my body is ballooning before your eyes, but if I catch you looking at anyone but me, you'll kill my self-esteem. And I might have to kill you.

- Do not try to win an argument. It's completely useless. In fact, surrender now and our lives will be so much easier. I know I'm not making a lot of sense right now, but try to remember that my body has been completely taken over and my mind is not my own. Take heart, I'll be back a few months after delivery.

- Do not deny me my cravings. Your logic will not convince me that I don't need ice cream or brownies or noodles *now.* Even if I claim to want a tin of sardines at three in the morning, you are well advised to get your cute ass to the store and get me some.

- Do not disregard my urgency to pee if you are the one driving the car. It's much easier to take five minutes and pull over at the gas station than to try to clean your nice leather seats.

- With the exception of my belly, which is supposed to be getting bigger and is supposed to be adorable to you, do not call attention to the other parts of my body that are getting bigger. Even if you think it's a compliment, I really don't need the man I love to tell me that my ass looks good with some meat on it.

- Do not hound me for sex when I am not in the mood (if I'm ever in the mood!). Go masturbate. I'm completely fine with that.

- Do not do anything that might awaken the Psycho Chick inside of me. That is, unless you have a compliment that I couldn't possibly misinterpret, don't provoke me with unprompted conversation.

- Don't ignore me when I'm blue. This may be more often than you think humanly possible, but remember that this is when I need a hug the most. Yours is the shoulder I most want to lean on.

A portion of the proceeds from the sale of this book will be donated to The Candies Foundation to support its mission to educate teens about the consequences of teenage pregnancy.
For more information, go to
http://www.candiesfoundation.org.